"Cook It, Spill It, Throw It
is an immersive,
one-of-a-kind experience in a world
we can't escape
(but let's face it, we don't want to!)."

—FROM THE FOREWORD BY

ANDY COHEN,

New York Times bestselling author,

host of Bravo's

Watch What Happens Live

with Andy Cohen

COOK IT, SPILL IT, THROW IT

COOK IT, SPILL IT, THROW IT

the not-so-Real Housewives *Parody Cookbook*

Stuart O'Keeffe and Amy Phillips

FOREWORD BY ANDY COHEN

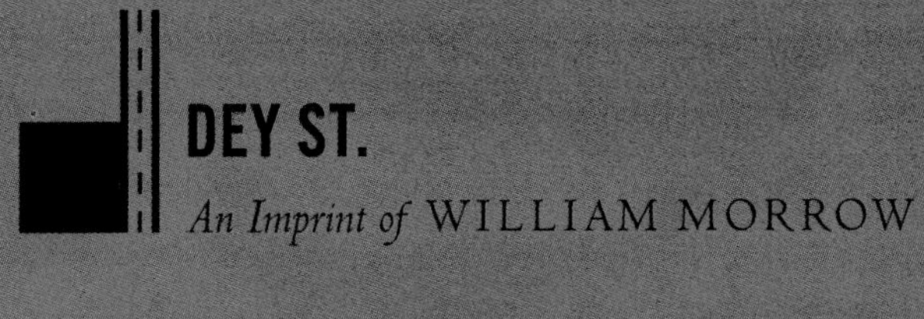

HarperCollins books may be purchased for educational, business, or sales promotional use. For information, please email the Special Markets Department at SPsales@harpercollins.com.

FIRST EDITION

Designed by Michelle Crowe

Arrow illustrations by Rebellion Works/ Shutterstock, Inc

All food photographs, unless credited otherwise below, are courtesy of Michael and Aline Hulswit.

Cover courtesy of Riker Brothers, as well as interior photos on pages 16, 18, 22, 26, 44, 54, 56, 62, 72, 94, 96, 108, 120, 122, 126, 132, 142, 145, 146, 172, 174, 182, 198, 218, 223, and 234.

Interior photography by Stuart O'Keeffe on pages 42, 90, 152, and 190.

Photographs of LaKendra Tookes are on pages 12, 22, and 228.

Library of Congress Cataloging-in-Publication Data has been applied for.

ISBN 978-0-06-303999-5

21 22 23 24 25 WOR 10 9 8 7 6 5 4 3 2 1

Stuart:

To my mom, Margaret O'Keeffe,
the realest housewife out there

To Baby Dawter

CONTENTS

FOREWORD

WHETHER YOU REALIZE IT OR NOT, FOOD PLAYS A VERY IMPORTANT role on *The Real Housewives*. For years we have purposely not edited out the ordering portion of the Wives' meals because we think what they eat says so much about who they are and how they interact with the world. I remember marveling at an early episode of *RHONJ* as Jacqueline Laurita ordered a steak at a diner and recall with fondness the time on *RHONY* when Sonja insisted Luann buy a blender to fuel her juicing obsession.

Think of how many key moments in the *Housewives* lexicon have involved food. A *cake* was the cause of blowouts in OC ("You took the BOW off my CAKE?!") *and* Jersey. In fact, if you close your eyes you can still hear Siggy Flicker freaking out about the destruction of the gorgeous cake she ordered for Melissa.

Jersey's roots were born in food: The ham game, sprinkle cookies, and Teresa's slam of Caroline in her cookbook all provided kindling for raging fires in the early years of the show. THE table flip happened at the dinner table. Beverly Hills's dinner party from hell happened after dinner. (By the way, what *did* Camille serve that night to make them all go hog wild?!?!)

Lest we forget about New York, the Big Apple was where we first heard about the "Skinnygirl margarita," and where we first met Lu and pondered eggs à la Française. Or the reverence we all have for Lisa Vanderpump's establishments.

With Comedian Amy and Chef Stuart at the helm, this tasty tribute to the *Housewives* that you currently hold in your hands is equal parts funny and delicious with a dash of irreverence, hold the lime. Whether it's a Toaster Oven Tart to commemorate Sonja's unique cooking habits, or a Henny-thing Can Happen cocktail for Porsha, the recipes contained in this book are hilarious, easy to prepare, and packed with jokes about each city, from Potomac to Beverly Hills.

This is all a long, blathering way of telling you that food makes up the fabric of *The Real Housewives*, and that it's so slyly brilliant that Amy and Stuart are bringing you closer to living like a Housewife through this book . . . or at least eating like one. *Cook It, Spill It, Throw It* is an immersive, one-of-a-kind experience in a world we can't escape (but let's face it, we don't want to!).

So if I might make a suggestion, why don't you roll up the sleeves of your QVC Lisa Rinna duster, pour yourself a stiff one, and crack open this book? Whether you decide to whip up a batch of Bunnygate Biscuits or catch yourself sloshing over Cease and Despritzer, I think you'll find yourself pleased with how decadent the drama tastes.

—**Andy Cohen,** *New York Times* bestselling author and host of Bravo's *Watch What Happens Live with Andy Cohen*

INTRODUCTION

BEYOND THE PERFECTLY SET TABLESCAPES, COUTURE-ADORNED ladies, the gossip and wine throws, lies the foundation for what brings together extraordinary groups of women: food. It's not about Botox, it's about brunch. Without dinner, there's no drama.

These heroic women and their spectacular side salads—and their side-eyes—are definitely different from most. For one, their uniforms are better (not to mention varying with each season). They demand to be addressed as members of the nobility, strut away after flipping tables, and can sometimes be heard referring to themselves as enigmas wrapped in riddles and cash. Sometimes, while wearing head-to-toe Versace and statement necklaces, they like to sling back a martini (or four) and issue choice words to other similarly bedecked women.

We're talking, of course, about the Real Housewives—the Lisas, the NeNes, the Sonjas and the Vickis, the Teresas and the Gizelles of this world. These ladies have been with us for over a decade now, appearing onscreen to entertain us with their hijinks, whether it's throwing prosthetic legs at parties or applying leeches to their bodies as beauty treatments.

They've also been generous enough to share valuable life lessons, teaching us that it's best to keep your legs closed to married men, and that if you have a dream—and enough money—you, too, can prove the naysayers wrong and release a studio single. Doesn't even matter if you're tone deaf!

We've embraced these heroes of their respective cities—not to mention American television. We pay homage to them in many ways: quoting their best sayings, drooling over their homes, and now, finally, by making *Housewives*-inspired meals. It feels fitting. After all, how many boozy breakfasts and catty cocktail hours have inspired some of the show's most epic moments? We remember that sisterly quarrel in a limo and a plate of food thrown across a table at an OC restaurant with fondness. All to say that food and drink drives the drama, yes, but it also brings the ladies together. When you think about it, food is fundamental to the *Housewives,* and much of the magic of the show happens at mealtime.

In *Cook It, Spill It, Throw It,* we aim to celebrate these women and their accomplishments, serving snacks with a little bit of snark. We raise our champs to these women, indubitably in the proper glassware, toasting them while ever so gently roasting them. It's all in good fun, of course!

But before you ask who would compile a full menu based on these women's antics, who could be brave enough to stare directly into the sun and attempt such a thing . . . well, we'll tell you: We're fans. Just like you. (Big fans. Maybe even superfans.) If these ladies have taught us anything, it's that you have to take pride in your passion—and you always show off the results at a dinner party.

Meet Stuart
THE CHEF

"If there's drama in my kitchen, it's because I stir the pot."

As a celebrity chef who has been cooking in restaurants and for A-list clients in LA for nearly two decades, I think it would be fair to say that my life can be just a *bit* hectic. Between hosting my own TV show, making on-air appearances as a food expert, and publishing a bestselling cookbook on easy-but-delicious home cooking, my life—you could even argue—is a *lot* hectic. Don't get me wrong—I love my life, but it isn't always made up of leisurely trips to the farmers' market and cute conversations over a cutting board. The stress of working sixteen-hour days in front of a hot stove (or camera) can really add up.

That's why on my craziest days, after I've finished overseeing a ten-course meal for a client, or taken my microphone off for the latest cooking segment with Rachael or Ted, I head home and make a beeline for my TV. The best way I know how to relax and not tear my own hair out is to watch my beloved Housewives tear each other's weaves out.

Give me Atlanta, give me New York and New Jersey and Orange County and Beverly Hills and Potomac and Dallas—I want them all. I've watched these women since the beginning (can you believe New York debuted in 2010?!), and with each season, as faces get tighter and Bethenny gets richer, my love for these ladies only grows.

It was on one of those late nights, with one eye on Bravo and the other on a pot of bubbling spaghetti, that I had a sudden flash of inspiration while watching the ladies of Beverly Hills go at it. As I watched yet another alcohol-soaked dinner party, I got so excited I almost let the spaghetti boil over. (I saved it just in time—I am a pro, after all.)

People love the Housewives, and they love to eat, I thought. *Why not combine the two?!* Wait, what? NO, I didn't mean eat them! Why would you think that? Ugh.

No, I thought, *what if there were a way to create hilarious recipes that honor the Housewives and make people laugh? Actually delicious recipes that send up the ladies' epic scuffles and eyebrow-raising zingers, yes, but ones that also acknowledge their undeniable savviness and smarts, as well as their many acts of charity and kindness?*

I knew I was on to something. The spaghetti hadn't even cooled before I was on the phone with Amy.

Meet Amy

"I may not be a Real Housewife, but I'm the realest fakest Housewife there is."

You might know me as "The Realest Fakest Housewife." But I need to "own it" and be "transparent" with you, I'm not actually an official Housewife, though I've been parodying them on radio, TV, and all over the Internet. Over the past decade I've made a living out of parodying the Real Housewives. I also have a Sirius XM show on "Daddy Andy's" very own channel, Radio Andy, where I recap each episode, and have the Housewives and other Bravolebrities on as my guests. Where does this obsession come from? It stems, of course, from a deep admiration for these sassy ladies and their perpetually thrilling lives. Also, have you ever put on a blond wig and sloshed a drink on your friends before? It's actually really fun. You should try it sometime.

Looking back, I suppose my appreciation for complex and hilarious personalities like the Housewives could be sourced all the way back to my middle school impressions of Liza Minnelli and Joan Rivers. I got just enough laughs to be encouraged, though, and eventually ended up leaving behind my hometown of Grosse Pointe, Michigan (not to mention my Midwestern accent!), to attend the American Academy of Dramatic Arts.

I then honed my comedy chops at The Second City and The iO Theater, before making my way to Los Angeles, where I eventually found myself a foremost expert on all matters related to the Housewives. Did I ever think my life would turn out this way? Well, let me pose a question to you: Do you think a certain New Jersey Housewife ever thought she'd go away to "camp" for a while?

Being deeply entrenched in every chapter of *Housewife* lore, from the nuances of the ladies' lawsuits to their lash extensions, I wasn't surprised that Stuart thought of me for partnering on a *Housewives* parody cookbook, though I sure was pleased. I knew we could make recipes as complex as their grudges and as juicy as their storylines. So, of course, I said yes to teaming up faster than a Housewife walking off a reunion stage. And now look where we are—at the dinner table with you!

SO HERE WE ARE, the savvy celebrity chef and the *Housewives* specialist coming together in a marriage fit for a limited series spinoff on Bravo, in the likes of Kim and Kroy, Kandi and Todd, or Bethenny and Jason. And because we are the experts, after all, we hope you'll trust us when we say that this book is the "thyme" and place to honor the paramount institution we call *The Real Housewives*. It's our hope that you'll have just as much fun reading and cooking from this book as we did in writing it. After all, we got to spend months reliving our favorite moments from the franchise and creating dishes inspired by some of the funniest, craziest, most unbelievable episodes. You want a tribute to Kenya's iconic reunion props? It's in here—mix yourself up a Scepter Peach Nectar Sangria. Or how about a love letter to Gizelle's favorite expression? We've got that, too, in the form of Word on the Street Corn. Still hungry for more? We also have Mention It Alllll-Fredo, Coto de Casserole, and Ponytail Pull-ed Pork for days, honey. In fact, we're pretty pleased with ourselves: No matter what your preferred flavor of drama is, we've got a recipe to match, for all the current (as of this writing) franchise cities: Atlanta, Beverly Hills, Dallas, New Jersey, New York, Orange County, and Potomac.

In addition to accessible, delicious recipes and jokes for days, you'll also find plenty of cooking tips and dinner party ideas to help you put together (and tear apart) a spread that would impress even a countess. And if you feel so inclined, you can document your good times online with #CookSpillThrow.

From feuds to lawsuits to vow renewals and everything in between, we capture it all in these dishes, made with a whole lotta love. Along the way, you will either become a Housewife-in-training or a pretty damn good cook—or perhaps both! And if you don't, well, "We're sorry you feel that way" and "Let's try to move forward." So uncork that bottle (or two) of red, unclip your hair extensions, and get cooking.

Recipe Key

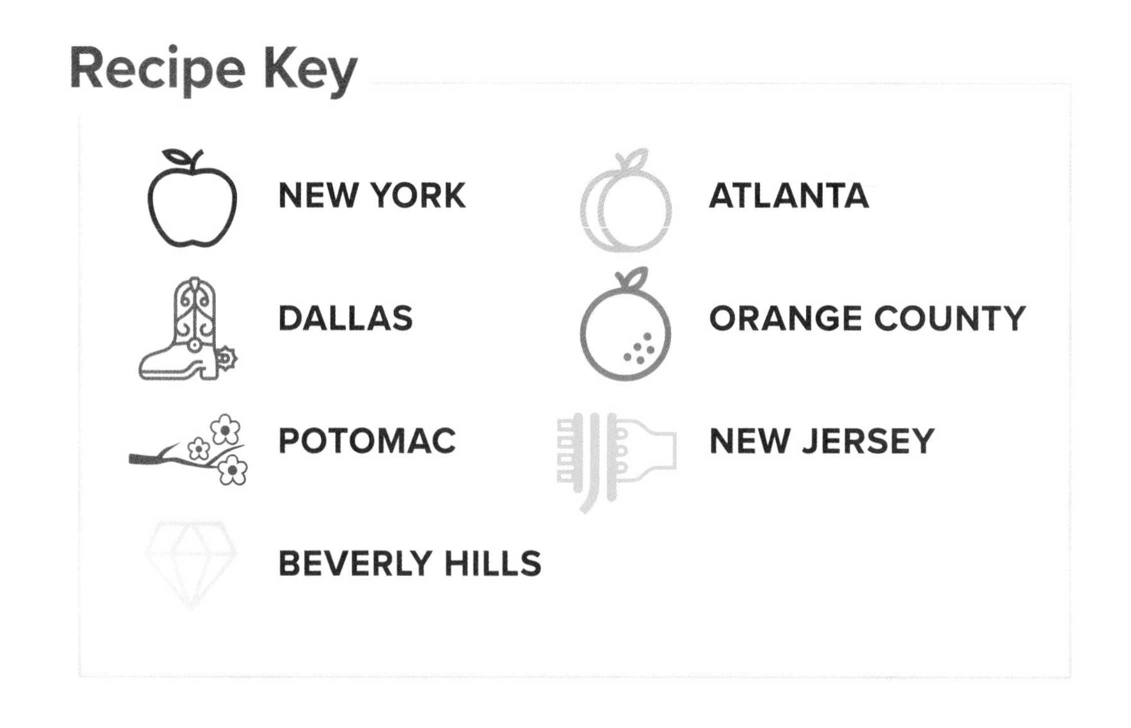

Stuart
Amy

PANTRY ESSENTIALS

HEY, HOW'S YOUR PANTRY? NOT WELL, BITCH? IT'S OKAY—WE KNOW it might be overwhelming when you don't have a full-time staff to stock your pantry shelves. Even if you're not working with the likes of Yolanda's fridge or Heather Dubrow's Champagne room, we're confident you can hold Housewife-level festivities and fights if you have the following necessities.

Pantry Must-Haves

- Extra-virgin olive oil
- Olive oil
- Kosher salt, preferably Morton
- Freshly ground black pepper
- Red wine vinegar
- Red pepper flakes
- Baking powder
- Cinnamon
- Vanilla extract
- Brown sugar
- Honey
- Powdered sugar
- Onion powder
- Garlic powder
- Dried oregano

- Canned San Marzano tomatoes
- Tomato paste
- Soy sauce
- Chicken stock
- All-purpose flour
- Granulated sugar
- Dried pasta
- Quick-cooking rice
- Sriracha sauce
- Yellow onions
- Fresh garlic

Tools (aka Your Kitchen's Glam Squad)

- 8-inch (20 cm) and 10-inch (25 cm) cast-iron skillets (Lodge is our favorite brand)
- Nonstick skillets (we recommend Circulon)
- 5-quart (4.7 l) Dutch oven (we love Le Creuset)
- Two 13 × 9-inch (33 × 23 cm) baking sheets (try OXO)
- Two 18 × 14-inch (46 × 36 cm) baking sheets (try OXO)
- Tongs, 1 large and 1 small (a combo of metal and silicone)
- Mixing bowls
- Measuring spoons
- Measuring cups
- Slotted spoon
- 2 silicone spatulas
- 2 wooden spoons
- 1 metal whisk
- 1 silicone whisk
- Ladle
- Microplane/rasp-style grater

Bar Basics

- Pinot Grigio
- Sauvignon Blanc
- Prosecco
- Mint sprigs
- Oranges
- Cocktail shaker
- Stainless steel jigger
- Champagne
- Vodka
- Limes
- Lemons
- Advil

One More Thing . . .

BEFORE YOU ORDER YOUR GROCERY DELIVERY, let's get this as clear as the pool water Tamra was baptized in, okay? We're serious about good food—we'd say we're just as committed to quality eats as Cynthia was to her 10/10/20 wedding date. But we don't want you to work harder than you have to; after all, a Housewife worth her margarita salt knows how to delegate. So if your housekeeper is on permanent vacation (read: you don't have one—neither do we!), we give you permission not to labor in the kitchen longer than you have to. Here and there throughout the book, we recommend store-bought ingredients. (Want to buy cake mix instead of baking from scratch? Use jarred tomato sauce? Do it!) We heartily approve of simple swaps or ingredient omittances if you can get away with it. Chef Stuart offers smart tips and tricks to cut down on cooking and cleanup time so you can pull off a magnificent spread fit for even the hangriest Housewife without breaking a sweat in your stilettos.

I AM VERY SHRIMP AND RICH BITCH GRITS
PAGE 27

BRUNCH

"Just because I start the day doesn't mean I can't finish it."

Here's the scene: You're hungover, you're regretting last night's decisions, and you may have to go on an apology tour like many of our treasured Housewives. We agree, brunch can be a bitch! But look no further for the ultimate meal that will make everything better. Eggs à Lu Française (page 17) can be the beginning to repairing a rift and our Dutch Baby Pancake with Yolanda Lemons (page 29) is sure to cushion the blow. So start with a Stick Wit Yer Blood-y Mary (page 205) and set the table for a brand-new day. And don't forget the Advil.

Table-Flipping Italian Frittata

Teresa flipped a table on Danielle so that one day we could flip frittatas for *you*. Basically, Teresa nearly knocked Danielle over when challenging her on her shady past, and we're going to knock out your taste buds with this incredibly yummy Italian-inspired breakfast. Like an infamous book packed full of saucy secrets, this Italian-style breakfast is bursting with sausage and veggies. You only need a few simple "ingrediences" for this. Perfect to make for your four "dorters."

SERVES 4 TO 6 **PREP TIME:** 15 minutes **COOK TIME:** 30 minutes **TOTAL TIME:** 45 minutes

---

¼ cup (60 ml) olive oil
½ medium onion, diced
2 cloves garlic, minced
8 ounces (220 g) Italian sausage, casings removed
1 medium zucchini, diced
8 large eggs
¼ cup (60 ml) heavy cream
½ teaspoon kosher salt
¼ teaspoon freshly ground black pepper
½ cup (45 g) grated parmesan cheese
You Stole My Goddamn House Salad (page 93)

Amy's Note: One bite of this and you'll be saying "Oh, Madonna mia!"

1. Preheat the oven to 400°F (200°C).

2. In a 10-inch (25 cm) ovenproof skillet, heat the oil over medium-high heat. Add the onion and cook until beginning to brown, about 3 minutes. Add the garlic and cook for 1 more minute. Set the onion/garlic mixture aside on a plate.

3. In the same skillet, cook the sausage over medium-high heat until cooked through, 3 to 4 minutes. Add the zucchini and cook until the zucchini is browned, 3 to 4 minutes more. Return the onion/garlic mixture to the pan and remove from the heat.

4. In a large bowl, lightly whisk together the eggs, cream, salt, and pepper. Add to the skillet and stir to combine. Top with the parmesan.

5. Transfer the skillet to the oven and bake until the eggs are set, 10 to 15 minutes. Remove and flip it onto a plate, place another plate on top, and flip once again like a table! Enjoy with You Stole My Goddamn House Salad.

Chef Stuart's Tip: You will know the eggs are cooked when the center of the frittata is no longer jiggly.

Eggs à Lu Française

Imagine the scene: a hungover beach morning in Turks and Caicos. Sonja had just mustered up the courage to tell Ramona and Bethenny that she was *not* an alcoholic when out of nowhere came Lu: "I made you eggs, à la Française," the Countess said. We give kudos to Sonja for standing up for herself, and say bravo to Luann, who made this untimely yet formal egg delivery the comedic relief we'll cherish forever. Enjoy this classic recipe while arguing on the beach, or in your breakfast nook wearing your favorite statement necklace.

SERVES 4 **PREP TIME:** 5 minutes **COOK TIME:** 5 minutes **TOTAL TIME:** 10 minutes

---

12 large eggs
¼ cup (60 ml) heavy cream
1 teaspoon kosher salt
¼ teaspoon freshly ground black pepper
4 tablespoons (60 g) unsalted butter
2 tablespoons chopped fresh chives
4 slices sourdough bread, toasted and buttered

1. In a large bowl, whisk together the eggs, cream, salt, and pepper until they start to become pale.

2. In a large nonstick skillet, heat the butter over medium heat until it begins to foam. Add the egg mixture and cook, stirring constantly with a spatula, until it begins to set (you want the eggs to be slightly wet, not dry), 2 to 3 minutes.

3. Stir in the chives. Remove from the heat and serve with the toasted sourdough.

Amy's Note: Make these eggs for your hungover friends. Come on, be cool, don't be all uncool.

Chef Stuart's Tip: As Luann would say, you're slowly stirring it all the time, and she means it, so do not step away!

Banana Xanax Smoothie

You don't have to have an iconic haircut or live in Beverly Hills to make an amazing smoothie, but it does help to have a sense of humor like our beloved Lisa Rinna's. In an unforgettable scene, Rinna had a show-and-tell with her bag of pills and made a joke about putting Xanax in a smoothie. The joke went *way* over Dorit's head and she made it a "thing" among the ladies. Don't worry, Rinna will seek revenge for this later, See Coke-Marinated Kebabs in the Bathroom (page 105). Sprinkle in cacao nibs in place of Xanax and you've got yourself one heck of an on-the-go breakfast.

SERVES 1 **PREP TIME:** 2 minutes **TOTAL TIME:** 2 minutes

---

1 large banana, cut into chunks
1 cup (140 g) ice
½ cup (120 ml) almond milk
¼ cup (70 g) plain Greek yogurt
2 teaspoons flaxseeds
2 teaspoons cacao nibs
1 tablespoon honey

In a blender, combine the banana, ice, almond milk, yogurt, flaxseeds, cacao nibs, and honey and blend until it's as smooth as Lisa's lips. Enjoy and OWN IT, PEOPLE! Own it!

Chef Stuart's Tip: I love to buy a few bananas, peel them, pop them in a zip-top freezer bag, and keep in my freezer to get an extra-cold smoothie.

Amy's Note: If this smoothie doesn't perk you up, turn on a Beverly Hills marathon and that will give you the serotonin boost you deserve. Also, we suggest taking a moment to give yourself a long, awkward Eden-style hug.

MUNCHAUSEN MIMOSA FOR BRUNCHAUSEN
PAGE 201

Eggs Brandi-dict with Hollman-daise

ON TEXAS TOAST

When you think of perfect pairs, you probably think of Brandi and Stephanie. This amazing duo bonds over pranks, farts, and Jesus Juice, and so in their honor we've added a new twist to another of our favorite duos: eggs and a gorgeous hollandaise sauce, featuring Texas toast. Not even a reality TV show could break up Brandi and Stephanie for good (unlike D'Andra and LeeAnne), and nothing will get between you and these eggs. Yeehaw!

SERVES 4 **PREP TIME:** 15 minutes **COOK TIME:** 10 minutes **TOTAL TIME:** 25 minutes

---

FOR THE POACHED EGGS

1 tablespoon distilled white vinegar
4 large eggs

FOR THE TEXAS TOAST

4 slices Texas toast or thick slices pain de mie bread
3 tablespoons (45 g) unsalted butter, at room temperature

FOR THE HOLLMAN-DAISE SAUCE

1½ sticks (6 oz/170 g) unsalted butter
3 large egg yolks
2 teaspoons fresh lime juice
1 teaspoon Worcestershire sauce
Pinch of cayenne pepper
Kosher salt and freshly ground black pepper

FOR SERVING

2 avocados, sliced
1 cup (260 g) store-bought mild salsa
Cilantro leaves, for garnish
Munchausen Mimosa for Brunchausen (page 201)

1. **MAKE THE POACHED EGGS:** In a saucepan bring 3 inches (7.5 cm) water and the vinegar to a simmer. Turn the heat off and add the 4 eggs at different spots in the pan so they are not touching. (It's easiest to crack eggs into 4 individual cups so you can slowly add to the water instead of cracking them straight into the water.) Cover the pan and let cook for 4 minutes. Using a slotted spoon, transfer the poached eggs to a plate lined with a paper towel to drain excess water.

2. **MEANWHILE, MAKE THE TOAST:** Toast the bread under the broiler and spread each with some butter.

3. **MAKE THE HOLLMAN-DAISE:** In a small saucepan, melt the butter over medium heat and set aside. In a blender or food processor, blend the egg yolks and lime juice together on low speed. With the blender on medium speed, add the hot melted butter, then add the Worcestershire sauce, cayenne, and a pinch each of salt and black pepper.

4. **TO SERVE:** Place a slice of buttered toast in the center of 4 plates, top with avocado slices and a drained poached egg. Top that with Hollman-daise, followed by some salsa. Garnish with cilantro leaves. Serve to your best friend and wash it all down with a Munchausen Mimosa.

Amy's Note: Share a bubble bath with your bestie and enjoy this brekkie.

Bloopberry Muffins

If you get read by NeNe, she will end it with her signature phrase: *Bloop!* It's truly one of the greatest *Housewives* catchphrases of all time and so addictive to repeat. These muffins are just as addictive because of their special crumbly tops. Warning, these muffins might make you thirsty so have something to drink because, as NeNe says, "The thirst is real."

MAKES 12 MUFFINS **PREP TIME:** 15 minutes **COOK TIME:** 25 minutes **TOTAL TIME:** 40 minutes

FOR THE CRUMB TOPPING

½ cup (65 g) all-purpose flour
3 tablespoons (45 g) cold unsalted butter, cut into ½-inch (1.25 cm) pieces
½ cup (100 g) granulated sugar

FOR THE MUFFINS

2 cups (260 g) all-purpose flour
¾ cup (150 g) granulated sugar
¼ cup (50 g) packed light brown sugar
1 teaspoon kosher salt
2½ teaspoons baking powder
½ cup (120 ml) vegetable oil
2 large eggs
½ cup (120 ml) whole milk
1 teaspoon vanilla extract
2 cups (200 g) blueberries
1 cup (320 g) blueberry jam

1. Preheat the oven to 400°F (200°C). Line 12 cups of a muffin tin with paper liners.

2. **MAKE THE CRUMB TOPPING:** In a bowl, combine the flour, butter, and sugar by rubbing the mixture with your fingers until you reach a crumb-like texture. Place the bowl in the fridge.

3. **MAKE THE MUFFINS:** In a large bowl, whisk together the flour, granulated sugar, brown sugar, salt, and baking powder.

4. In a separate large bowl, mix the oil, eggs, milk, and vanilla.

5. In three batches, mix the wet ingredients into the bowl of dry ingredients. Stir to combine. Fold in the blueberries.

6. Fill each muffin cup one-third with batter. Spoon a teaspoon of blueberry jam on top and cover with more batter.

7. Sprinkle the crumb topping over the muffin batter and bake until the muffin tops bounce back up when pressed with your index finger, 20 to 25 minutes. Let cool for 10 minutes before serving. Store in an airtight container.

Amy's Note: When you are adding the blueberries it's imperative that you drop them into the batter one by one and say *bloop! bloop! bloop!* Trust me, you do it once and it'll become "the new normal!"

Bunnygate Biscuits

Remember when Kim decided that Rinna's stuffed bunny gift for her grandson was just bad energy? Well, we're making up for that with these mouthwatering good-energy bunny biscuits; they're so good you can't help but feel positive. Even though Rinna owned what she said about Kim being an enabler (not to mention near-death!), it wasn't enough for Kim to keep the bunny. We bet if Rinna had had these warm, buttery biscuits to offer Kim, she might have been able to fix the damage and skip those award-winning reunion tears. If you're an overachiever or a "hustler," put a honey "tear" detail on these bunnies before serving.

MAKES 6 BUNNY BISCUITS **PREP TIME:** 15 minutes **COOK TIME:** 10 minutes **TOTAL TIME:** 25 minutes

---

1 (16 oz/450 g) can refrigerated buttermilk biscuits
12 raisins, for eyes
24 slivered almonds
3 red candied cherries, halved, for noses
1 teaspoon honey, for tears

Amy's Note: Just like Kim, I am superstitious (about food), so I'm certain that these biscuits will bring good energy to any party.

1. Preheat the oven to 350°F (175°C). Line an 18 × 14-inch (46 cm × 36 cm) baking sheet with parchment paper.

2. Lay 3 full biscuits on a work surface. Turn your knife on the flat side and slice each biscuit through the middle lengthwise. Now you have 6 round pieces. Slice each round in half through the middle. Now you have 12 pieces for the ears. Place 2 ears under a full biscuit and pinch to adhere the ears to the bunny head. Transfer each bunny to the baking sheet.

3. Press 2 raisins as eyes onto each biscuit. Place 4 slivered almonds on each biscuit, to make whiskers. Bake until lightly browned all over, about 10 minutes.

4. Let cool and place a half cherry as the nose on each biscuit.

5. Drizzle a few tear-shaped drops of honey just below one or both of the eyes on each bunny.

Chef Stuart's Tip: When you've graduated from the bunny slopes, go beyond canned biscuits and try making this recipe with my homemade Butter Knife Brawl Biscuits (page 30).

I Am Very Shrimp and Rich Bitch Grits

Shrimp and grits are both staples of a Southern diet, and when you put them together, it's like NeNe and Shereé—the most glorious combination ever. This riveting moment between NeNe and Shereé was all about the Benjamins. Shereé whisked up her issues with NeNe when she accused her of taking money out of her pocket, but NeNe wasn't having it and let her know that she was "cashing Trump checks" and that she was "very rich, bitch." Much like this unforgettable scene, this meal will stick with you for a while—and the bacon will add the sizzle that a dramatic moment needs.

SERVES 4 **PREP TIME:** 10 minutes **COOK TIME:** 30 minutes **TOTAL TIME:** 40 minutes

---

1 teaspoon kosher salt
½ teaspoon freshly ground black pepper
1 cup (260 g) white corn grits
2 cups (480 ml) whole milk
1 cup (85 g) shredded sharp cheddar cheese
2 tablespoons (30 g) unsalted butter
5 thick-cut slices bacon, chopped
1 pound (460 g) shrimp, peeled and deveined
1 teaspoon paprika
2 cloves garlic, chopped
1 tablespoon chopped fresh parsley
Juice of 1 lemon

1. In a large saucepan, bring 2 cups (480 ml) water to a boil. Season the boiling water with the salt and pepper and pour in the grits, whisking as you pour. Whisk in the milk and cook over medium heat according to package directions. Stir in the cheddar and butter. Remove from the heat and set aside.

2. Meanwhile, in a large nonstick skillet, cook the bacon over medium heat until browned, 5 to 6 minutes. Remove from the heat and set aside on a plate lined with a paper towel.

3. In a bowl, season the shrimp with the paprika. Add them to the bacon grease in the skillet and cook over medium heat until they turn pink, 2 to 3 minutes. Stir in the garlic, cooked bacon, parsley, and lemon juice. Remove from the heat.

4. Spoon the grits into the center of a large dinner plate and spoon the bacon/shrimp mixture on top. Serve. If you don't have napkins, feel free to use some Benjamins!

Amy's Note: This dish is done, honey, just like NeNe's new teeth.

Chef Stuart's Tip: If your grits are, well, gritty, and too chewy, try adding a bit of water and cooking for longer until they reach your desired texture.

Dutch Baby Pancake with Yolanda Lemons

Hello, my love! We know it's not technically in the dictionary, but "lemon" is actually synonymous with "Yolanda." It's just a fact. This fan-favorite Housewife once planted fifty lemon trees at her home, but the orchard yielded so many lemons she didn't know what to do with them. Well, here's an idea: Make a glorious, indulgent pancake. This recipe is inspired by Yolanda's beautiful home country of the Netherlands. Et voilà—our favorite Dutch Housewife inspires our favorite Dutch delicacy.

SERVES 4 **PREP TIME:** 10 minutes **COOK TIME:** 25 minutes **TOTAL TIME:** 35 minutes

---

3 large eggs
½ cup (120 ml) half-and-half
1 teaspoon vanilla extract
Grated zest of 1 lemon
½ cup (65 g) all-purpose flour
¼ cup (50 g) granulated sugar
5 tablespoons (75 g) unsalted butter
1 tablespoon powdered sugar, for dusting
2 cups (380 g) fresh mixed berries
Maple syrup, for drizzling

1. Preheat the oven to 425°F (220°C).

2. In a medium bowl, whisk together the eggs, half-and-half, vanilla, and lemon zest.

3. In a large bowl, combine the flour and sugar. Add the egg mixture to the dry ingredients and mix well.

4. In a 10-inch (25 cm) cast-iron skillet, melt the butter over medium heat. Add the batter to the pan, transfer to the oven, and bake until browned and set, about 20 minutes. Turn off the oven and let the pancake sit in the oven for 5 minutes more to finish baking.

5. Remove from the oven, dust with powdered sugar, cut into wedges, and serve with the berries and syrup, while saying in your best Dutch accent, "Hello, my luhv! Here are some lemon pancakes for *yooooooou*!"

Amy's Note: Full disclosure, this dish is not part of the "Master Cleanse."

Chef Stuart's Tip: Be sure to use a 9- or 10-inch (23 cm or 25 cm) skillet. The smaller pan will give added puffiness to your pancake!

Butter Knife Brawl Biscuits

IN MOMMA'S HOUSE GRAVY

The butter knife threat heard 'round the world happened in Candiace's house—well, some say, in Candiace's *momma's* house. This drama took place during a tasting party for Chef Chris's cookbook (how meta because now it's in our cookbook). Candiace lost her scruples while wielding a butter knife in the air at Ashley, but her unhinged behavior inspired an undeniably delicious meal. These biscuits are so soft and flaky you won't need a butter knife to cut through them, but you'll need a *lot* of buttermilk to make them. Paired with this rich gravy, even Ashley would agree that this dish is worth getting kicked out for, over and over again.

MAKES 12 BISCUITS **PREP TIME:** 20 minutes **COOK TIME:** 30 minutes **TOTAL TIME:** 1 hour 10 minutes (includes 20 minutes chilling time)

FOR THE BISCUITS

- 2½ cups (320 g) all-purpose flour, plus more for the work surface
- ¼ cup (50 g) sugar
- 1 tablespoon baking powder
- ¾ teaspoon baking soda
- 1 teaspoon kosher salt
- 1 stick (4 oz/115 g), plus 3 tablespoons (50 g) unsalted butter, cold
- 1½ cups (360 ml) buttermilk
- Egg wash: 1 large egg whisked with 1 teaspoon water

1. Preheat the oven to 450°F (230°C). Line a 18 × 14-inch (46 × 36 cm) baking sheet with parchment paper.

2. **MAKE THE BISCUITS:** In a large bowl, whisk together the flour, sugar, baking powder, baking soda, and salt. Using a sharp knife, roughly chop up the butter into small pieces and toss them into the flour mixture. Alternatively, pulse the flour mixture in a food processor until the mixture forms a crumb-like texture, 8 to 10 pulses, and transfer the mixture to a large bowl.

3. Pour the buttermilk into the flour and mix using a wooden spoon or spatula until it all clumps together.

4. Dust a work surface generously with flour and using the heels of your hands press out the dough into a rectangle roughly 5 × 12 inches (12 × 30 cm) and ¾ inch (2 cm) thick. Sprinkle with flour and fold into thirds. Repeat the pressing and folding three more times. Finally, press out the dough to a 10-inch (25 cm) square.

5. Using a 3-inch (8 cm) cutter, cut out rounds. Flip them over and place on the lined baking sheet. Gather up all the scraps, press to the same thickness, and cut out more rounds. Dust off excess flour. Refrigerate the biscuits for about 20 minutes, until chilled.

6. Brush the tops of the biscuits with the egg wash.

FOR THE GRAVY

1 pound (460 g) breakfast sausage, casings removed
1 teaspoon fresh thyme, chopped
4 tablespoons (60 g) unsalted butter
¼ cup (35 g) all-purpose flour
2½ cups (600 ml) whole milk

7. Bake until golden, 16 to 18 minutes Let cool on a wire rack.

8. MEANWHILE, MAKE THE GRAVY: In a large skillet, cook the sausage and thyme over medium heat until the sausage is cooked through and lightly browned, 5 to 8 minutes. Remove and set aside.

9. In the same pan, melt the butter over medium heat, sprinkle with the flour, and whisk until it forms a paste. Add the milk, bring to a simmer, and cook for about 2 minutes to thicken. Mix in the sausage.

10. To serve, split the biscuits in half, place two halves on a plate, top each with 2 to 3 tablespoons of gravy, and enjoy.

Chef Stuart's Tip: Any leftover biscuits? Serve them with Eggs à Lu Française (page 17).

Amy's Note: It's so good, the flavor smacks you in the face like a purse!

Forgotten Truffle Frois

The only way to say fries is with Ramona's heavy New York accent: "frois." Remember when their fries were forgotten that day at the beach? Who knew that Sonja would spiral after joining Luann at a Miami AA meeting, causing the ladies' beach day to be cut short?! They packed up and took the food to go. But after they regrouped at the house, the ladies discovered that the establishment forgot to give them the truffle fries! The women were beyond distraught and Bethenny called the incident "egregious." Now not only will you always pronounce fries with Ramona's New York accent, you'll want those "frois" as badly as they did.

SERVES 4 **PREP TIME:** 20 minutes **COOK TIME:** 30 minutes **TOTAL TIME:** 50 minutes

---

2 pounds (900 g) russet potatoes
3 cups (720 ml) vegetable oil
1 tablespoon sea salt, plus more to taste
2 tablespoons good truffle oil
½ cup (45 g) grated pecorino cheese
2 tablespoons chopped fresh parsley

Amy's Note: Miami forgot the "frois," but we sure didn't! To be enjoyed after AA or while admiring your *Cabaret* poster.

1. Preheat the oven to 200°F (90°C). Line one 18 × 14-inch (46 × 36 cm) baking sheet with parchment paper.

2. Cut the potatoes into long sticks, ½ inch (1 cm) thick. Lay out the sticks on some paper towels and pat to dry completely.

3. In a 10-inch (25 cm) cast-iron skillet over medium heat, heat the vegetable oil to 300°F (150°C). Cook a handful of potato sticks for 5 minutes at this heat. Use a candy thermometer to keep the temperature accurate, raising or lowering the heat if necessary. Set the fries aside on paper towels and repeat with the remaining potato sticks. Let cool for 10 minutes.

4. Increase the heat of the oil to 350°F (175°C) and cook the fries again in batches for 2 to 3 minutes or until lightly browned. Repeat with the remaining fries. Cooking the fries twice gives them a crispy exterior and a fluffy interior.

5. Place the fries on the baking sheet and keep warm in the oven.

6. When ready to serve, toss the fries with the sea salt, truffle oil, pecorino, and parsley.

7. Sprinkle with more sea salt if needed. (It would be egregious to have undersalted "frois"!)

Chef Stuart's Tip: Pat those potatoes dry as much as you can—moisture is what gives you a soggy (or "sawwgy" in Ramona speak) fry.

FUNCTION
START/CANCEL
TEMP
Darkness
TIME

Toaster Oven Tarts

The toaster oven that never came to be is finally given its due with our tart recipe to honor our sweet Sonja. Don't worry if you don't have a toaster oven, you can still make these in a conventional oven—so long as you first don your pearls and loafers with your family crest.

SERVES 4 **PREP TIME:** 20 minutes **COOK TIME:** 10 minutes **TOTAL TIME:** 1 hour (includes 30 minutes to set the icing)

¾ cup (150 g) packed light brown sugar
1 teaspoon ground cinnamon
1 teaspoon cornstarch
1 (14 oz/400 g) box refrigerated pie crusts
1 large egg
1 teaspoon whole milk

FOR THE ICING

1 cup (120 g) powdered sugar
1 tablespoon whole milk
½ teaspoon vanilla extract

1. Preheat the oven or toaster oven to 425°F (220°C). Line an 18 × 14-inch (46 × 36 cm) baking sheet with parchment paper. If using a toaster oven, you will need two 12 × 9-inch (30 × 23 cm) trays lined with parchment paper.

2. In a bowl, combine the brown sugar, cinnamon, and cornstarch together. Set aside.

3. Unroll both pie crusts and square the edges of each. Cut each crust into four rectangles. Place 1 tablespoon of the brown sugar mixture in the center of a rectangle and spread almost to the edge, leaving a ¼-inch (½ cm) border, and top with another rectangle of dough. Crimp the edges with a fork to seal. Repeat with the remaining rectangles. Poke holes in the tops of each tart with the same fork so the steam can escape. In a small bowl, whisk together the egg and milk. Brush the tops of the tarts with the egg wash. Transfer the tarts to the baking sheet.

4. Bake the tarts until lightly browned, 8 to 10 minutes. Transfer to a wire rack to cool completely.

5. **MEANWHILE, MAKE THE ICING:** In a small bowl, stir together the powdered sugar, milk, and vanilla.

6. Spread the icing on top of the cooled tarts and let set for 30 minutes to 1 hour before enjoying.

Chef Stuart's Tip: Crush some fresh berries like raspberries or blueberries to replace the cinnamon/brown sugar filling. Just don't overfill or they'll leak!

SPARKLE DOGS
PAGE 55

APPETIZERS

"I can be passed, but no one ever takes a pass on me."

Much like the friends of the Housewives add dimension to the show, appetizers add dimension to a meal. Think about it: You don't realize how much you appreciate a Marlo, a Kim D., or a Kim G. until they pop in and stir up the drama. They never hold back, and for this, we thank them for their service. Break out your most beautiful appetizer platter and pass the Morally Corrupt Satay Res-sticks (page 41). These apps can be the stars of the show if you let them—and believe us, they deserve it!

What Are You Doing Here Without Deviled Eggs

The ladies of New York are little devils when it comes to nightlife, mixing and mingling at their local haunts all over the Upper East Side. Tipsy Girl Sonja ran into Dorinda's boyfriend, John, at the Housewives' hotspot Beautique and wasted no time demanding why he was there without Dorinda. No night is complete without drama for these ladies, and no party you go to is complete without deviled eggs, so clearly you need this recipe.

MAKES 12 DEVILED EGGS **PREP TIME:** 20 minutes **COOK TIME:** 10 minutes **TOTAL TIME:** 30 minutes

---

6 large eggs
3 tablespoons mayonnaise
2 teaspoons hot sauce
1 teaspoon Dijon mustard
1 teaspoon chopped fresh dill
½ teaspoon kosher salt
¼ teaspoon freshly ground black pepper
1 tablespoon chopped fresh chives, for garnish
Paprika, for garnish

Amy's Note: With this app, you'll always have the greatest niiiiiight!

1. Place the eggs in a saucepan and add enough cold water to cover. Bring to a boil over medium-high heat, then remove from the heat, cover, and let sit for 10 minutes. Transfer the eggs to a bowl of ice water and let cool for 5 minutes.

2. Peel the eggs and carefully cut them lengthwise. Using a small spoon, remove the yolks and place them in a bowl. Add the mayo, hot sauce, mustard, dill, salt, and pepper and mash until super smooth.

3. Spoon the mixture into a zip-top plastic bag, cut one corner off, and pipe the mixture into the egg white shells. Garnish with chives and a sprinkling of paprika to make it nice.

Chef Stuart's Tip: If you have any leftover yolk mixture, toast some bread and spread it on top for a tasty snack!

The Morally Corrupt Satay Res-sticks

Camille skewered and grilled Faye over her scandalous spread in *Playboy* magazine, and we skewer and grill these savory chicken satays for our prized "friend of" Kyle, Faye Resnick. If you recall, The Dinner Party from Hell was the perfect opportunity for Camille to put Faye on blast for being morally corrupt for posing naked after she testified as a witness in the OJ trial. The irony is that Camille posed in *Playboy* as well, and believe us, the hypocrisy smells as sweet as this sauce. Dare we say, they both looked fabulous!

SERVES 4 **PREP TIME:** 10 minutes **COOK TIME:** 20 minutes **TOTAL TIME:** 2 hours 30 minutes (includes 2 hours marinating time)

FOR THE MARINATED CHICKEN

- ⅔ cup (160 ml) canned full-fat coconut milk
- ¼ cup (60 ml) reduced-sodium soy sauce
- 1 tablespoon curry powder
- 1 teaspoon ground turmeric
- 4 cloves garlic, minced
- 2 tablespoons (30 g) packed light brown sugar
- 1 tablespoon fish sauce
- 2 teaspoons toasted sesame oil
- ½ teaspoon kosher salt
- ¼ teaspoon freshly ground black pepper
- 2 pounds (900 g) boneless, skinless chicken thighs, cut into 2-inch (5 cm) pieces
- Eight 8-inch (20 cm) wooden skewers
- Cilantro leaves
- ½ cup (75 g) peanuts, roughly chopped
- 2 limes, cut into wedges

FOR THE SPICY PEANUT SAUCE

- ½ cup (150 g) smooth peanut butter
- 1 tablespoon soy sauce
- 2 tablespoons fresh lime juice
- 1 tablespoon light brown sugar
- 1 teaspoon sriracha sauce

1. **MARINATE THE CHICKEN:** In a gallon-size zip-top plastic bag, combine the coconut milk, soy sauce, curry powder, turmeric, garlic, brown sugar, fish sauce, sesame oil, salt, and pepper. Add the chicken, seal, and toss in the bag for 1 minute. Transfer to the fridge to marinate for 2 hours.

2. Remove the chicken from the bag and pat with paper towels to remove some of the marinade. Thread 3 pieces of chicken onto each of the skewers.

3. **MAKE THE SPICY PEANUT SAUCE:** In a bowl, whisk together the peanut butter, soy sauce, lime juice, brown sugar, and sriracha (move that whisk like Camille dancing in Vegas). If the sauce is too thick, add some water to thin it. Set aside. (If you're feeling "pernicious," add an extra dash of sriracha.)

4. Set a grill pan or cast-iron skillet over medium-high heat.

5. Cook the chicken until it registers 165°F (75°C) on a thermometer, about 3 minutes per side.

6. Stack the skewers on a platter, sprinkle with cilantro, chopped peanuts, and a squeeze of lime juice. Serve with the peanut sauce.

Amy's Note: Faye says she didn't "spread," but we encourage you to spread the sauce all over the chicken to achieve flavor throughout.

Hit a Nerve Herb and Tomato Bruschetta

Our quick-witted blonde Jersey Housewife is not one to back down to anyone, and if you want a taste of Margaret's wrath, this app is for you—just take a big bite like when Margaret bit into both bruschetta and Jen during an al fresco dinner one night. Yes, you heard right: After making an accusation that Jen's husband sleeps in the pool house, Margaret nonchalantly asked Jen, "Hit a nerve?" before breaking into her bruschetta. The insult landed and hit Jen like a bomb. Margaret didn't have a care in the world, but *we* cared, so we made a bruschetta app that is perfect for any party. Hopefully it only hits the good nerves . . .

SERVES 4 **PREP TIME:** 10 minutes **COOK TIME:** 10 minutes **TOTAL TIME:** 40 minutes (includes 20 minutes marinating time)

---

1 baguette
2 tablespoons extra-virgin olive oil, plus more for brushing
Kosher salt and freshly ground black pepper
6 Roma (plum) tomatoes, diced
½ teaspoon garlic powder
10 fresh basil leaves, chopped
¼ cup (60 ml) balsamic vinegar
½ cup (45 g) shaved parmesan cheese

1. Preheat the oven to 350°F (175°C).

2. Trim both ends off the baguette, split it horizontally, then halve crosswise for a total of 4 pieces. Halve crosswise again for 8 pieces.

3. Arrange the pieces of bread cut side up on a baking sheet, drizzle each with some of the oil, and lightly season with salt and pepper. Bake until lightly toasted, 8 to 10 minutes. Set aside.

4. In a bowl, combine the tomatoes, garlic powder, basil, balsamic, and the 2 tablespoons oil. Let sit for 20 minutes to marinate.

5. Lay the toasts on a platter and top generously with the tomato mixture. Sprinkle the parmesan on top. Serve.

Amy's Note: Insults are welcome before munching on these tasty bites, specifically that someone's lip liner looks like a "monkey's asshole." It's very Jersey.

Chef Stuart's Tip: Want even more flavor? Let the tomatoes marinate overnight.

I Fly Above, Kandied Wings

No one has built an empire like Kandi Burruss. From music (our obvious favorite is "I Fly Above"), writing, acting, and restaurants, to producing sex toys and cosmetics, she has truly "Kandied" up everything in her path. Well, we candied up these wings to make them as hot and sweet as Kandi. There's no drama with this recipe. "Don't start none, won't be none."

SERVES 4 **PREP TIME:** 15 minutes **COOK TIME:** 35 minutes **TOTAL TIME:** 1 hour 10 minutes (includes 20 minutes marinating time)

- Vegetable oil, for deep-frying
- 3 pounds (1.4 kg) chicken wings
- ¼ cup (130 g) cornstarch
- 1 teaspoon kosher salt
- ¼ teaspoon freshly ground black pepper

FOR THE SAUCE

- ¾ cup (180 ml) Thai sweet chili sauce
- ¼ cup (60 ml) fresh orange juice
- 1 tablespoon reduced-sodium soy sauce
- 1 teaspoon cornstarch

FOR SERVING

- ¼ cup (40 g) toasted sesame seeds
- 2 scallions, thinly sliced

Amy's Note: Fly above the drama with these wings because they will make your taste buds soar.

1. Pour at least 3 inches (7 cm) of oil into a large Dutch oven or heavy-bottomed pot and heat over medium heat to 350°F (175°C). Use a candy thermometer to maintain a consistent temperature.

2. Meanwhile, pat the chicken wings dry with a paper towel. In a large bowl, toss the wings with the cornstarch, salt, pepper, and 1 tablespoon water. Let sit for 20 minutes to marinate while the oil comes to temperature.

3. **MAKE THE SAUCE:** In a small saucepan, combine the sweet chili sauce, orange juice, soy sauce, and cornstarch. Bring the sauce to a simmer over medium heat and cook for 3 to 5 minutes to thicken. Transfer to a large bowl and set aside.

4. Working in batches of 5 to 7 wings, use tongs to carefully lower them into the hot oil and fry until golden brown, crispy, and fully cooked, 7 to 10 minutes. Set aside on a baking sheet and cover with foil to keep warm.

5. Place all the cooked chicken wings in the large bowl with the sauce and toss until coated.

6. Arrange on a large platter and sprinkle with the sesame seeds and scallions. Enjoy! Grab the napkins!

Chef Stuart's Tip: Don't skip drying the chicken wings, as this step will give you a crispier wing! Moisture is not your friend when frying.

WE GOT THE YACHT SHOTS

PAGE 236

Tardy for the Party Mix

Kim Z. wasn't the first Housewife to put out a single, but she sure made her mark with one of the greatest songs in *Housewives* history. With the producing brilliance of Kandi Burress, "Tardy for the Party" is the gold standard for a Housewife bop, even though the song caused rifts between Kim and NeNe, *and* Kim and Kandi. Despite Kim's music career coming to a halt after two songs, thanks to her spin-off show her reality TV career has gone on to be wildly successful. This party mix is perfect for family night or binge-watching *Don't Be Tardy.*

SERVES 6 TO 8 **PREP TIME:** 10 minutes **COOK TIME:** 10 minutes **TOTAL TIME:** 20 minutes

---

1 stick (4 oz/115 g) unsalted butter
4 teaspoons Worcestershire sauce
1 teaspoon garlic powder
1 teaspoon onion powder
1 cup (150 g) roasted cashews
1 cup (150 g) peanuts
1 cup (100 g) pretzel sticks
1 cup (50 g) bagel chips, broken into 1-inch (2.5 cm) pieces
2 cups (50 g) Corn Chex cereal

Amy's Note: Kim wouldn't be caught dead without a red Solo cup, so scoop this snack in one and enjoy with white wine.

1. Preheat the oven to 425°F (220°C).
2. In a small saucepan, melt the butter over medium heat. Stir in the Worcestershire sauce, garlic powder, and onion powder.
3. In a large bowl, combine the cashews, peanuts, pretzel sticks, bagel chips, and Corn Chex. Pour in the butter mixture and toss with two spatulas to combine very well. Spread evenly on an 18 × 14-inch (46 × 36 cm) baking sheet.
4. Bake until light golden brown, 8 to 10 minutes.
5. Serve in multiple red plastic cups for your party!

Word on the Street Corn

Have you heard the word on the street? It's that this corn is as charming and zingy as former First Lady of the church Gizelle Bryant. Just like an episode of Potomac wouldn't be complete without Gizelle's signature phrase, you'll find your dinner is no longer complete without this corn dish. Rumor has it that this version of street corn is sweet, spicy, and deliciously messy—just like Gizelle.

SERVES 4 **PREP TIME:** 10 minutes **COOK TIME:** 25 minutes **TOTAL TIME:** 35 minutes

---

2 tablespoons olive oil
4 ears corn, husked
½ cup (120 g) sour cream
⅓ cup (80 g) mayonnaise
1 cup (200 g) crumbled Cotija cheese, plus more for garnish
1 teaspoon ground cumin
½ teaspoon chili powder, plus more for garnish
1 jalapeño, seeded and finely chopped
1 scallion, finely chopped
½ cup (10 g) cilantro, finely chopped, plus leaves for garnish
2 limes, cut into quarters

1. In a large cast-iron skillet, heat 1 tablespoon of the oil over medium heat. Add 2 ears of the corn and cook until they turn bright yellow with char marks on them, 8 to 10 minutes. Repeat with the remaining 1 tablespoon oil and corn. (Alternatively, brush the ears with oil and cook the corn on the grill until nice and charred.)

2. Meanwhile, in a large bowl, combine the sour cream, mayo, ¾ cup (150 g) of the Cotija, the cumin, and chili powder. Pour onto a plate.

3. Roll the corn in the creamy dip. Place on a platter. Sprinkle with the jalapeño, scallion, cilantro, more chili powder, and the remaining Cotija. Squeeze fresh lime juice over the dressed corn. Enjoy!

Amy's Note: Get ready to roast your corn like Gizelle roasts her friends.

5 Good Summers Carole-viche

Princess Carole's journey on RHONY was ride or die, honey. We watched her be besties with Bethenny, break up with Bethenny, have a relationship with Adam, break up with Adam, write a book (no ghostwriter, by the way), cut her hair, change her wardrobe drastically, and even run a marathon. Throughout her journey, Carole had a "best-selling" way with words—and sure enough the words struck us when she told Bethenny that she only has five good summers left. Carole, trust us, you have many more good summers left to enjoy your cool downtown life. And there is no better summer appetizer than this refreshing summer ceviche.

SERVES 4 TO 6 **PREP TIME:** 20 minutes **COOK TIME:** 30 minutes (in the fridge) **TOTAL TIME:** 50 minutes

---

- ¾ pound (340 g) shrimp, peeled and deveined
- Juice of 2 lemons
- Juice of 2 limes
- 1 cup (200 g) cherry tomatoes, quartered
- ¼ medium red onion, finely chopped
- 1 small jalapeño, finely chopped
- 2 teaspoons chopped fresh cilantro
- ½ teaspoon garlic powder
- ½ teaspoon kosher salt
- 2 avocados, diced
- Tortilla chips, for serving

Amy's Note: Make sure you eat it all because we'll be looking for "What Remains" on your plate.

1. Remove the tails from the shrimp and discard. Cut the shrimp into small bite-size pieces.

2. In a large bowl, combine the lemon juice, lime juice, tomatoes, red onion, jalapeño, cilantro, garlic powder, and salt. Stir in the shrimp and refrigerate for 30 minutes.

3. Just before serving, toss the avocado with the shrimp. Serve in martini glasses with several tortilla chips. See how easy this is? If you're like Carole and you converted your kitchen into an office, don't worry, you can still make it!

Chef Stuart's Tip: If you don't want to "cook" the raw shrimp in the juices, just boil the shrimp in water for 3 minutes then cut into bite-size pieces and toss together with the remaining ingredients.

Pillow Fight Popcorn Chicken

Pop this popcorn chicken because this scene had us watching on the edge of our seats—or shall we say our pillows! NeNe hosted a couples' night that she called "Pillow Talk," where they played a game called "How well do you know your mate?" But even amid their lingerie attire and sprawling-pillow décor, things really went sour. Pillows and fists were thrown, leaving all the couples irate. It was like watching a sexy action film!

SERVES 4 **PREP TIME:** 20 minutes **COOK TIME:** 30 minutes **TOTAL TIME:** 50 minutes

---

FOR THE SEASONING MIX

1 teaspoon curry powder
1 teaspoon smoked paprika
1 teaspoon onion powder
1 teaspoon garlic powder
1 teaspoon kosher salt
½ teaspoon chili powder
½ teaspoon freshly ground black pepper

FOR THE CHICKEN

1 pound (500 g) boneless, skinless chicken breasts
¼ cup (30 g) cornstarch
1 cup (240 ml) buttermilk
1½ cups (180 g) panko bread crumbs
2 cups (480 l) vegetable oil, for frying

FOR SERVING

L'Infinity Dress-ing (page 95) or ranch dressing (from Who Gon' Check Me Blue Cheese Buffalo Dip, page 63)

1. **MAKE THE SEASONING MIX:** In a large bowl, toss together all the spices.

2. **PREPARE THE CHICKEN:** Cut the chicken into bite-size pieces (about 2 inches/5 cm). This will help them cook evenly.

3. Add the chicken to the bowl of seasoning mix and toss well to coat. Add the cornstarch and toss again.

4. Set two bowls on the counter, one filled with the buttermilk and the other with the bread crumbs. Dip each chicken piece into the buttermilk and then into the bread crumbs and set on an 18 × 14-inch (46 × 36 cm) baking sheet. Repeat with all the chicken pieces.

5. In a large heavy pot over medium heat, heat the oil to 350°F (175°C). Use a candy thermometer to maintain a consistent temperature.

6. Place the chicken gently into the hot oil, about 10 pieces at a time, and cook until golden brown, 3 to 5 minutes, gently stirring so they don't stick to the bottom of the pan. Line another 18 × 14-inch (46 x 36 cm) baking sheet with paper towels. Remove the cooked chicken from the pot and place on the paper towels to drain excess oil. Repeat with the remaining pieces of chicken.

7. Serve on a pillow with L'Infinity Dress-ing or ranch dressing.

Amy's Note: Don't be mad at us, NeNe, because we're getting up out of our goddamn seat to make these poppers!

Sparkle Dogs

Gurl, gurl, gurl, you are gonna love these party dogs! You don't even have to have a tiny dog to enjoy these. Inspired by Kameron's dream to produce the first-ever premium pink dog food—aka SparkleDog—we felt compelled to make pink corn dogs. Just like Kam dressed up her Yorkshire terrier Louis in designer fashions, we adorned these dogs with a special pink sauce and sprinkles. These are like dog treats for adults . . . so consider them human treats!

FOR THE DOGS

3 cups (720 ml) vegetable oil, for deep-frying
1 cup (120 g) white cornmeal
1 cup (130 g) all-purpose flour
⅓ cup (70 g) sugar
2 tablespoons baking powder
½ teaspoon kosher salt
Pinch of freshly ground black pepper
1 large egg
1 cup (240 ml) whole milk
Red food coloring
Six 6-inch (15 cm) wooden skewers
Six 5-inch (13 cm) beef hot dogs

FOR THE PINK SAUCE

½ cup (120 g) ketchup
¼ cup (60 g) mayonnaise

Amy's Note: Some were concerned that SparkleDog food would make dogs poop pink, and thus we feel the same concern about our pink corn dogs . . . so, let us know what happens.

1. **MAKE THE DOGS:** Pour 3 inches (8 cm) oil into a deep 10-inch (25 cm) cast-iron skillet or Dutch oven and heat over medium heat to 350°F (175°C). Use a candy thermometer to maintain a consistent temperature.

2. While the oil is coming to temperature, in a medium bowl, combine the cornmeal, flour, sugar, baking powder, salt, and pepper. In another medium bowl, whisk together the egg and milk. Add the egg mixture to the dry ingredients and mix well to combine. Add a small drop of red food coloring to the batter and slowly stir it in to make the mixture pink. Add more if needed.

3. Insert a skewer into each hot dog.

4. Pour the batter into a tall glass, leaving about 2 inches (5 cm) from the top of the glass. Dip a hot dog into the batter and then lower into the hot oil and fry until golden, 2 to 3 minutes; turn over every 30 seconds using metal tongs until light and golden all over. Set aside on a plate lined with paper towels. Repeat with the remaining hot dogs.

5. **MAKE THE PINK SAUCE:** In a small bowl, combine the ketchup and mayo until the sauce turns a lovely pink color. Place in a small zip-top bag, snip one corner with scissors, and drizzle over the finished dogs. Serve warm.

Chef Stuart's Tip: Go easy with the food coloring: We want a pink, not a deep red color. Less is more.

Wow, Bethenny, Bao

A tribute dish to a phrase we've heard Ramona say many times and that we have not grown tired of saying ourselves: "Wow, Bethenny, *wow.*" When you are stuffing the *bao,* make sure to open them as wide as Ramona's mouth when she was appalled by Bethenny's brutally honest remarks. We know one thing for sure, we support Bethenny's honesty as much as Ramona's anti-aging skincare line—and we hope they support this yummy Asian-inspired sandwich.

SERVES 6 TO 8 **PREP TIME:** 2 hours **COOK TIME:** 30 minutes **TOTAL TIME:** 2 hours 30 minutes (includes 2 hours rising time)

FOR THE BAO BUNS

2 cups (270 g) all-purpose flour, plus more for dusting
1 cup (136 g) cornstarch
5 tablespoons superfine sugar
1 teaspoon instant yeast
2½ teaspoons (10 g) baking powder
1 cup (240 ml) warm water (86°F/30°C)
¼ cup (60 ml) vegetable oil, plus more for rubbing

FOR THE FIVE-SPICE PORK

½ cup (120 ml) hoisin sauce
1 teaspoon reduced-sodium soy sauce
1 tablespoon rice vinegar
2 tablespoons light brown sugar
1 teaspoon Chinese five-spice powder
2 teaspoons olive oil
1 pound (450 g) boneless pork chops, cut into thin strips

1. **MAKE THE BAO BUNS:** Measure the flour, cornstarch, sugar, yeast, and baking powder into the mixing bowl of a stand mixer fitted with the dough hook. In a measuring cup, combine the water and vegetable oil.

2. Add the wet ingredients into the mixing bowl, set to medium speed, and let mix for 10 minutes. Place the dough on a floured surface and knead for 5 minutes.

3. Place the dough into a clean bowl and cover with a kitchen towel. Let it rest in a warm spot for 90 minutes until doubled in size. I like to turn on my oven to 175°F (85°C) and switch it off and place the bowl in there.

4. **MEANWHILE, START THE FIVE-SPICE PORK:** In a small saucepan, combine the hoisin sauce, soy sauce, vinegar, brown sugar, and Chinese five-spice. Set over medium heat and stir for 2 to 3 minutes to dissolve the brown sugar. Set aside.

5. Place the dough on a surface dusted with flour and punch and knead for 5 minutes to release any air bubbles.

6. Roll out the dough until ½ inch (1.5 cm) thick. Rub some oil on the surface of the dough.

7. Use a 3- or 4-inch (10 cm) cookie cutter to cut out rounds from the dough. Rub some more oil on the cut pieces and place them on an 18 × 14-inch (46 × 36 cm) baking sheet lined with parchment paper. Reroll out the remaining dough and continue cutting rounds until no dough is left.

recipe continued on page 58

FOR SERVING

1 cup (110 g) shredded carrot
¼ red onion, thinly sliced
1 tablespoon rice vinegar
1 teaspoon granulated sugar
2 teaspoons sesame seeds
1 Fresno chile or jalapeño pepper, thinly sliced
1 cup (20 g) cilantro leaves

8. Place the rounds onto 4 x 4-inch (10 x 10 cm) pieces of parchment paper, or you can use flattened-out cupcake liners.

9. Place all the buns on a large tray, cover with a kitchen towel, and leave in a warm place for another 30 minutes for the buns to rise again. They will puff up.

10. MEANWHILE, CONTINUE WITH THE PORK: In a large nonstick skillet, heat the olive oil over high heat, add half the pork strips and stir-fry until cooked through, 3 to 5 minutes. Remove from the skillet. Repeat with the remaining pork. Return all the pork to the pan along with the reserved sauce and keep warm over low heat.

11. COOK THE BUNS: Set up a steamer (preferably with more than one tier) over boiling water. Place 2 buns and their parchment squares on each tier and steam until puffed up and smooth, 10 to 12 minutes. Repeat with the remaining buns.

12. In a small bowl, toss together the carrot, red onion, vinegar, and sugar; set aside.

13. TO ASSEMBLE AND SERVE: Open up the buns, fill each with 2 to 3 pieces of pork, and top with the sesame seeds, pickled carrot-onion mixture, chile slices, and some cilantro leaves.

Chef Stuart's Tip: These buns can be made up to a day ahead, and you can pop them in the microwave for 20 seconds to warm them up before serving.

Drag Brie Monique, Drag Brie

Candiace was a few wines in when she tempted Monique with the question of "dragging" her. Now, we don't condone putting your hands on anyone, so instead we encourage you to "drag" your apple slices, crudités, and bread through this melty baked goodness. A wine tasting event that left us speechless will now leave you delightfully breathless as you indulge in the tastiest app that is perfect for your own wine tasting party. This one brings enough drama on its own, so take the lawsuits off the table and replace them with this dish. The only fight happening here will be who gets more of this savory cheesy goodness.

SERVES 4 TO 6 **PREP TIME:** 5 minutes **COOK TIME:** 20 minutes **TOTAL TIME:** 25 minutes

---

1 (8 oz/225 g) wheel of Brie
2 tablespoons honey
½ cup (75 g) toasted walnuts, roughly chopped
¼ cup (40 g) pistachios
¼ cup (30 g) dried cranberries
3 Medjool dates, pitted and chopped
1 teaspoon minced fresh rosemary
Baguette slices and crackers, for serving

1. Preheat the oven to 350°F (175°C). Line an 18 × 14-inch (46 × 36 cm) baking sheet with parchment paper.

2. Place the Brie on the baking sheet and bake for 20 minutes.

3. Meanwhile, in a bowl, mix together the honey, walnuts, pistachios, cranberries, chopped dates, and rosemary.

4. Remove the Brie from the oven and place in the center of a round platter. Spoon the fruit and nut mixture on top of the cheese wheel. Place baguette slices and crackers around the cheese on the board. Drag those crackers through that Brie!

Amy's Note: This Brie is so good that Ashley is willing to make a statement about it to help Monique's case against Candiace.

5-Story Townhouse Dip

PREPARED BY INTERNS

Sonja's historic home has seen it all, from "panty soup" to toaster-oven meals and a revolving door of Housewives and interns. Despite its faults—be they leaky pipes, a broken elevator, or an eternally defective toilet—the townhouse has kept its charm and mystique longer than the Morgan family letters have been around. The good news is that the five-floor townhouse is lauded in our five-layer dip, and it won't cost $50K a month to keep up! Serve to your socialite friends or enjoy solo with your poodle while sitting in your four-poster canopy bed. Wearing a tiara, of course.

SERVES 6 TO 8 **PREP TIME:** 15 minutes **TOTAL TIME:** 25 minutes (includes 10 minutes assembly time)

---

3 avocados, halved and pitted
Juice of 1 lime
½ medium onion, minced
1 clove garlic, minced
Kosher salt and freshly ground black pepper
2 cups (245 g) sour cream
1 tablespoon taco seasoning
2 large tomatoes, seeded and diced
2 teaspoons chopped fresh cilantro
2 cans (32 oz/900 g) refried beans
1 cup (80 grams) shredded Mexican cheese blend
½ cup (90 g) sliced black olives
Tortilla chips, for serving

1. Scoop the avocado flesh into a medium bowl. Add the lime juice, onion, and garlic, and season with salt and pepper to taste. Mash everything together and set the guacamole aside.

2. In a small bowl, mix together the sour cream and taco seasoning. Set aside.

3. In another bowl, combine the tomatoes, cilantro, and salt and pepper to taste. Set aside.

4. In a 7¼-inch diameter × 3¼-inch high (18 cm × 8 cm) glass bowl, make layers in this order (bottom to top): refried beans, guacamole, taco-seasoned sour cream, tomato mixture, and cheese.

5. Top with the olives and have your interns serve the dip with tortilla chips.

Amy's Note: You won't lose a tooth eating these dips! Serve with a side of "Pickles" in honor of Sonja's favorite intern.

Who Gon' Check Me Blue Cheese Buffalo Dip

One of the most memorable lines from Atlanta came about when a sit-down business meeting between Shereé and her party planner exploded into a stand-up face-off. Shereé is not one to be intimidated by anyone, so when the party planner got spicy with her, she challenged him with the question, "Who gon' check me, boo?" The party they were planning was to celebrate Shereé's independence, aka divorce, but after seeing her get the upper hand in this situation, we think she had her independence long before the divorce was finalized. We turned this epic face-off into a Buffalo sauce for your face.

SERVES 6 TO 8 **PREP TIME:** 20 minutes **COOK TIME:** 20 minutes **TOTAL TIME:** 40 minutes

---

FOR THE RANCH DRESSING

½ cup (130 g) sour cream
¼ cup (60 g) mayonnaise
¼ cup (60 ml) buttermilk
Juice of ½ lemon
1 teaspoon dried parsley
½ teaspoon garlic powder
½ teaspoon kosher salt
¼ teaspoon onion powder
¼ teaspoon freshly ground black pepper

FOR THE BUFFALO DIP

10 ounces (300 g) cream cheese, at room temperature
¾ cup (70 g) blue cheese crumbles
3 cups (420 g) shredded rotisserie chicken
1 cup (240 ml) Frank's RedHot sauce
2 cups (200 g) shredded mozzarella cheese

FOR SERVING

1 (10 oz/285 g) bag bagel chips or 1 baguette, thinly sliced and toasted
4 medium carrots, cut into 4-inch (10 cm) sticks
4 stalks celery, trimmed and cut into 4-inch (10 cm) sticks

1. Preheat the oven to 375°F (190°C).

2. **MAKE THE RANCH DRESSING:** In a medium bowl, whisk together the ranch dressing ingredients. Refrigerate until needed.

3. **MAKE THE BUFFALO DIP:** In a bowl, mix together the cream cheese, ¼ cup of the blue cheese, the chicken, hot sauce, and 1 cup of the mozzarella. Spread on the bottom of a 9-inch (23 cm) square baking dish or a round cast-iron pan. Top with the remaining 1 cup mozzarella and remaining ½ cup blue cheese crumbles.

4. Bake until nice and bubbling, about 20 minutes.

5. Serve the Buffalo dip with the bagel chips or toasted baguette slices, carrots, celery, and the ranch dressing.

Amy's Note: Jam out to Shereé's song of this name and serve at a divorce celebration or an Atlanta premiere party.

Clip Clip Clip Medley of Dips Dips Dips

Dorinda is known for her ballsy attitude and clever comebacks. In true fashion, she once invented a new way to shut someone up—aka to "clip" them. These Italian-inspired dips will remind you of the time the New York ladies went to an Italian trattoria in the Bronx and a fight broke out over whether Dorinda wanted to be a part of Tipsy Girl. Dorinda rebuked Sonja's accusation by vehemently gesticulating and yelling, "Clip clip clip!" Enjoy a dip for every "clip."

Romesco Dip

SERVES 4 **PREP TIME:** 12 minutes **COOK TIME:** 3 minutes **TOTAL TIME:** 15 minutes

- ½ cup (55 g) slivered almonds
- 1 (14 oz/400 g) jar roasted red bell peppers
- ¾ cup (170 g) tomato paste
- ½ cup (10 g) fresh Italian flat-leaf parsley
- 2 cloves garlic, peeled
- ½ cup (120 ml) extra-virgin olive oil
- Juice of 1 lemon
- ½ teaspoon kosher salt
- Flatbread or toasted baguette slices, for serving

1. In a small dry skillet, toast the almonds over medium heat until lightly browned, 3 to 5 minutes. Let cool, then transfer to a food processor.

2. Add the roasted peppers, tomato paste, parsley, garlic, oil, lemon juice, and salt to the food processor and blend until smooth. If the dipping sauce seems too thick, add water 1 teaspoon at a time to thin.

3. Serve with flatbread and/or toasted baguette slices.

Chef Stuart's Tip: Romesco sauce originated in northern Spain, but we've taken some creative liberties to hearken to Italy with this dip. Buon appetito!

Amy's Note: You better bring these dips to a party or you better "back it up!"

Chef Stuart's Tip: Try topping chicken or fish with Romesco sauce—*delizioso*!

Walnut Pesto

SERVES 4 **PREP TIME:** 5 minutes **COOK TIME:** 5 minutes **TOTAL TIME:** 10 minutes

1 cup (115 g) walnuts
2 large cloves garlic, roughly chopped
2 cups (40 g) fresh basil leaves
½ teaspoon kosher salt
¼ teaspoon freshly ground black pepper
¾ cup (175 ml) extra-virgin olive oil
½ cup (45 g) grated parmesan cheese
Toasted baguette slices and crackers, for serving

1. In a medium dry skillet, toast the walnuts over medium heat for 3 to 5 minutes, stirring constantly so that you toast all sides of the nuts. Let cool slightly, then transfer to a food processor.

2. Add the garlic, basil, salt, and pepper and pulse 5 to 10 times. With the machine running, slowly stream in the oil and add the parmesan incrementally while continuing to blend.

3. Serve in a dipping bowl with plenty of toasted baguette slices and crackers.

Rosemary and Garlic White Bean Dip

SERVES 4 **PREP TIME:** 10 minutes **COOK TIME:** 10 minutes **TOTAL TIME:** 20 minutes

⅓ cup (80 ml) extra-virgin olive oil, plus more for garnish
8 cloves garlic, roughly chopped
1 sprig rosemary, leaves picked
2 (15 oz/425 g) cans cannellini beans, drained and rinsed
½ teaspoon kosher salt
¼ teaspoon freshly ground black pepper
Juice of 1 lemon
Toasted baguette slices and crackers, for serving

1. In a medium saucepan, heat the oil and garlic over medium-low heat for 2 to 3 minutes. Add the rosemary leaves and cook for another 1 to 2 minutes.

2. In a food processor, pulse the cannellini beans, salt, pepper, and lemon juice together. Add the olive oil/garlic/rosemary mixture and blend together until well combined.

3. Transfer to a bowl for serving and drizzle with some oil to garnish. Serve with plenty of toasted baguette slices and crackers.

Tres Amigas 3-Layer Dip

Whether it's racing golf carts, swimming in their Spanx, or doing shots in sombreros, these three Orange County ladies love to have layers and layers of fun. We made this delightful dip with one layer for Vicki, one layer for Tamra, and one layer for Shannon. You decide which is which. Cry into your nachos or get on the bar and dance like you're at Andalés, we won't judge!

SERVES 4 **PREP TIME:** 5 minutes **COOK TIME:** 20 minutes **TOTAL TIME:** 25 minutes

---

1 (8 oz/225 g) package cream cheese, at room temperature
2 cups (500 g) store-bought salsa
1½ cups (125 g) shredded Mexican cheese blend
Tortilla chips, for serving

1. Preheat the oven to 350°F (175°C).
2. Spread the cream cheese on the bottom of an 8-inch (20 cm) nonstick round pan or baking dish. Top with the salsa and sprinkle with Mexican cheese blend.
3. Bake until the cheese is bubbling, about 20 minutes.
4. Serve with tortilla chips.

Chef Stuart's Tip: Ramp up your store-bought salsa with a shot of tequila to really get the party going with this super-easy dip.

Charcuterie Tray “On Display”

This charcuterie board has all the bells and whistles, much like Melissa’s first stage performance of her hit Housewives single “On Display.” Joe built her a studio to record this song. This was blk. water’s first launch event and all family and friends (including our favorite Greg Bennett) were there watching, so needless to say the stakes were high. Even though Joe didn’t get tigers for her show, she delivered an epic performance. Not only is this charcuterie board gorgeous like Melissa but it makes the perfect appetizer or light dinner for any occasion. Don’t be afraid to flip the cheese into the air like Melissa, when you’re “down the shore.”

SERVES 4 TO 6 **PREP TIME:** 10 minutes **TOTAL TIME:** 30 minutes

---

FOR THE CHEESES

8 ounces (225 g) sharp cheddar, cut into 2-inch (5 cm) pieces
11 ounces (310 g) goat cheese log
8 ounces (225 g) blue cheese
8 ounces (225 g) Manchego cheese

FOR THE MEATS

½ pound (225 g) prosciutto
½ pound (225 g) mortadella
¼ pound (113 g) salami

FOR THE CRACKERS/ BREAD

A variety of crackers
1 French baguette, sliced and toasted

FOR THE FRUIT

Green grapes
Medjool dates
Green olives
Dried cranberries
Fig jam

FOR THE NUTS

Candied walnuts or pecans
Sesame honey cashews or dry roasted cashews

1. Grab a large wooden or marble cutting board. Line a baking sheet with parchment paper and place all the cheeses on the tray.
2. Follow the picture on page 71 as your guide to create this masterful platter, using the meats, crackers, bread, fruit, and nuts, or get creative and put your own spin on it!

Amy’s Note: This will be the “Envy” of any party. Put this “On Display.” Thank you, Jesus!

Chef Stuart’s Tip: There's no wrong way to DISPLAY this delicious charcuterie board—have fun with it and wash it down with blk. water.

Paramus Palace Party Platter

Can you see Paramus from Jennifer Aydin's mountaintop home? You sure can. Can you get a feel for Jen's big personality and ornate mansion through this exceptional app? We sure hope so. This Housewife was always ready to share her family life and Turkish heritage with us, and what better way to celebrate than with a shareable platter of delicious food? Pull up a throne, relax, and channel your inner Jennifer. Seriously, just throw the utensils across the table; you won't need them for these finger foods.

SERVES 8 TO 10 (NOT QUITE AS MANY SERVINGS AS JEN'S 16 BATHROOMS) **PREP TIME:** 15 minutes **COOK TIME:** 30 minutes **TOTAL TIME:** 1 hour 15 minutes (includes 30 minutes assembly time)

Spiced Chickpeas

- 1 (14 oz/400 g) can chickpeas, drained and rinsed
- 1 tablespoon extra-virgin olive oil
- 2 cloves garlic, minced or grated
- ½ teaspoon chili powder
- ½ teaspoon ground cumin
- ½ teaspoon onion powder
- 1 teaspoon dried oregano

1. Preheat the oven to 400°F (200°C). Line a sheet pan with parchment paper.

2. In a bowl, toss together all the ingredients. Pour the mixture onto the pan and bake until crispy, 20 to 30 minutes.

Simple Hummus

- 1 (14 oz/400 g) can chickpeas, drained and rinsed
- ½ cup (120 ml) extra-virgin olive oil
- 2 cloves garlic, peeled
- 1 teaspoon fresh lemon juice
- ¼ cup (65 g) tahini
- 1 teaspoon kosher salt
- ½ teaspoon freshly ground black pepper

In a food processor, combine all the ingredients and process to a puree. If the hummus seems too thick, add water 1 teaspoon at a time to loosen it up.

For Serving

- Lavash bread (or crackers)
- Toasted pita bread
- Olives
- Feta cheese
- Marcona almonds
- Tabbouleh (store-bought)
- Cucumbers cut into sticks, 3-inch (7 cm) sticks
- Sun-dried tomatoes
- Medjool dates

All you have to do is arrange the food and you're good to go. (Check out the photo on page 70.) Now go enjoy the view of Paramus!

Amy's Note: Don't be afraid to mix these Turkish nibbles together like an arranged marriage. And for tequila lovers like Jen, we suggest pairing with a Sonjarita (page 209)!

DRAG BRIE MONIQUE, DRAG BRIE
PAGE 59

GORGA-ZOLA BALLS
PAGE 117

WHAT ARE YOU DOING HERE W[illegible]HOUT

PARAMUS PALACE

Party Platter

TRASH SPRINKLE COOKIES
PAGE 185

MY MOTHA'S PIZZELLE
PAGE 195

CHARCUTERIE TRAY "ON DISPLAY"
PAGE 68

DUBROW-KEN BOW CHAMPAGNE CUPCAKES
PAGE 171

DIAPER DUMP CAKE
PAGE 177

SANDWICHES, SOUPS, AND SALADS

"I'm more than just a snack, I'm the whole meal!"

We're not afraid to get our hands dirty, like Kim Richards when she made a special chicken salad for her daughter. And we have no problem putting in our time, like when "Ramonja" escaped a clam bake with a swag bag of hard-won lobsters. Soups, salads, and sandwiches are not always the most glamorous, but they work hard, dammit, just like the Housewives do when they dedicate their time to soup kitchens and fundraising events. After all, Shannon "starts charities," didn't you know? These soups and salads will go the distance in satisfying those hunger pangs when you're craving something a little simpler but still delicious.

BIG CHICKIM SALAD SANDWICH
PAGE 77

Big ChicKim Salad Sandwich

Don't be afraid to get your hands dirty, because it's a must when you're making a homemade chicken salad using Kim's signature hand-tossed method. It may not be common practice to walk around your house mixing a salad with your hands, but rules are made so that Housewives can break them. And in the cooking world, this scene gave us a lot of inspiration. As Kim's daughter Kimberly was getting her hair and makeup done for prom, Kim took care to make things special for her big night. She made lemonade, put out hors d'oeuvres, and made her famous chicken salad. The cameras weren't shy about zooming in on Kim chopping the chicken, apples, and walnuts, and then stirring it all into a giant bowl . . . with her hands. Kim gave Kimberly a special rosary for the night and we give you this very blessed salad.

SERVES 4 **PREP TIME:** 20 minutes **TOTAL TIME:** 30 minutes (includes 10 minutes assembly time)

½ cup (120 g) mayonnaise, preferably Best Foods or Hellmann's
2 teaspoons fresh lemon juice
1 teaspoon kosher salt
½ teaspoon freshly ground black pepper
3 cups (420 g) shredded rotisserie chicken
1 cup (150 g) walnuts, roughly chopped
½ cup (65 g) dried cranberries
2 stalks celery, finely chopped
1 red apple, diced
1 tablespoon chopped fresh tarragon
8 slices multigrain bread
8 leaves butter lettuce

1. In a large bowl, whisk together the mayo, lemon juice, salt, and pepper.

2. Add the chicken, walnuts, cranberries, celery, apple, and tarragon and toss together with your bare hands while walking around the house.

3. Place 4 slices of bread on the work surface and top each with a lettuce leaf. Add on a generous portion of chicken salad and a second slice of bread.

4. Bless the sandwiches with a rosary and serve one to your prom date.

Chef Stuart's Tip: Although this recipe serves 4 people, you can triple the recipe to make the portion Kim made in that episode. And sadly, though no one ate Kim's salad, I am certain someone will eat yours. This salad keeps for 3 days in the fridge in an airtight container.

Ham-sterdam Grilled Cheese, You Beast

Are we talking about Kim's drinking *again*, ladies? Well, Kim wasn't having it and turned up the heat in Amsterdam by insinuating something negative about Lisa Rinna's husband, causing Rinna to go "ham" and throw a wineglass. Kyle quickly fled, crying in a cape. And of course we'll never forget Kim calling sweet Eileen a "beast." What a scene! Well, for this beast of a sandwich we use Gouda cheese from Yolanda's homeland of the Netherlands. Now the secret's out on how to make an outstanding grilled sandwich.

SERVES 4 **PREP TIME:** 10 minutes **COOK TIME:** 20 minutes **TOTAL TIME:** 30 minutes

---

8 tablespoons (120 g) unsalted butter, at room temperature
8 slices sourdough bread
¾ cup (60 g) grated pecorino cheese
½ cup (120 g) Dijon mustard
12 thin slices ham
8 slices Gouda cheese
12 dill pickle slices
Potato chips, for serving

Amy's Note: Let's not talk about the husband, but let's talk about this amazing grilled cheese.

1. Spread 1 tablespoon butter on each slice of bread. Sprinkle the pecorino onto a plate and press the buttered side of each bread slice onto the cheese. Set the bread cheese side down on a cutting board.

2. Spread mustard on all the slices of bread. Top 4 of the mustard-covered slices with 3 slices of ham, 2 slices of Gouda, and 3 pickle slices each. Top the sandwiches with the remaining 4 slices of bread, placing the mustard side down onto each sandwich.

3. Heat a large nonstick skillet over medium heat. Place a sandwich on the hot surface, cover with a sheet of wax paper, and place a cast-iron skillet or heavy pan on top. Brown for 2 to 3 minutes, then flip over and brown the other side. Repeat with the remaining sandwiches.

4. Cut in half and serve with potato chips and a glass of wine to throw.

Lobster TO GO Tartine

It's safe to say that Barbara's iconic clambake got off to a wacky start. For starters, not all of the ladies were invited—most notably, Dorinda. And the other women who attended didn't stay at Barbara's for long before Tinsley's alarm went off, signaling they should head back to Ramona's house to save Dorinda from *Law & Order* reruns. Bethenny, being the *Housewives* soothsayer she is, predicted that Ramona would put clams in a tote bag. In fact she wasn't that far off. Sonja scooped up some lobsters in her Sonja Morgan New York white lace dress while Ramona shoved three or four in her bag. They had their eyes on the seafood prize, and similarly we award this salad to you, "Ramonja!"

SERVES 4 **PREP TIME:** 10 minutes **TOTAL TIME:** 15 minutes

---

- 3 tablespoons mayonnaise
- 1 tablespoon fresh lemon juice
- 1 tablespoon extra-virgin olive oil
- 1 tablespoon chopped fresh tarragon
- ½ teaspoon onion powder
- ½ teaspoon kosher salt
- ¼ teaspoon freshly ground black pepper
- 3 lobster tails, fully cooked and cut into 1-inch (2.5 cm) chunks
- 1 cup (180 g) cherry tomatoes, halved
- ½ English cucumber, finely diced
- 1 head butter lettuce
- 4 slices brioche bread, toasted
- 1 avocado, diced
- 2 scallions, thinly sliced

1. In a large bowl, mix together the mayo, lemon juice, oil, tarragon, onion powder, salt, and pepper. Fold in the lobster meat along with the tomatoes and cucumber.

2. Place a few lettuce leaves on each slice of brioche and top with some lobster salad. Garnish with the avocado and scallions.

Chef Stuart's Tip: If you choose to buy fresh lobster tails, they will take about 1 minute per ounce to cook in boiling water.

Amy's Note: I can confidently say, like Sonja, I'm not leaving this lobster tartine, that's who I am, that's just *who I am*.

There's a Cougar Burger on the Loose in the OC

When a great *Housewives* tagline is born it shines as bright as the sun. Kelly Dodd's Season 13 tagline brought a lot of entertainment in one simple line: "Call animal control, cuz there's a cougar on the loose in the OC." Now, this method of chasing meat won't get animal control called on you, but, hey, eating a good California burger *is* an animalistic experience.

SERVES 4 **PREP TIME:** 20 minutes **COOK TIME:** 10 minutes **TOTAL TIME:** 1 hour 15 minutes (includes 45 minutes resting time)

FOR THE BURGERS

1½ pounds (680 g) ground beef (80 to 85% lean)
1 teaspoon kosher salt
½ teaspoon freshly ground black pepper
Cooking spray
2 tablespoons yellow mustard
4 slices American cheese
2 cups (150 g) shredded iceberg lettuce
4 hamburger buns
4 slices red onion
4 tomato slices

FOR THE COUGAR SAUCE

3 tablespoons tomato ketchup
2 tablespoons mayonnaise
2 tablespoons sweet pickle relish
1 teaspoon fresh lemon juice

Forgotten Truffle Frois (page 33), for serving

1. **MAKE THE BURGERS:** Remove the beef from the fridge and let rest for 45 minutes to come to room temperature.

2. Divide the beef into 4 portions and form each into a patty 1 inch (2.5 cm) thick. Season both sides with salt and pepper. Using your index finger, press an indentation in the center of each patty.

3. **WHILE THE BEEF IS RESTING, MAKE THE COUGAR SAUCE:** In a small bowl, whisk together the ketchup, mayo, relish, and lemon juice. Set aside.

4. Heat a large skillet over medium-high heat. Mist the pan with cooking spray. Add the patties to the pan and cook for 3 to 4 minutes, brushing each patty with ½ tablespoon of the mustard before you flip. Flip and cook for another 3 to 4 minutes. Top each patty with a slice of cheese.

5. Place the shredded lettuce on the bottom half of each bun, top with a cooked patty, a tablespoon or so of cougar sauce, an onion slice, tomato slice, and finally the top half of the bun. Enjoy with some Forgotten Truffle Frois.

Amy's Note: Don't turn your back on this cougar burger or it will eat you alive like Kelly, you little dork, twerp b*&$ch!

Ponytail Pull-ed Pork

You should never put your hands on somebody! Instead, put your hands on these scrumptious pulled pork sandwiches. When Margaret poured water on Danielle's head and all over her Versace outfit we didn't know it would turn into the boutique fight from hell. Again, we don't condone violence, *but* you'll need to get physical to pull apart this pork like Danielle pulled Margaret's pony. Go ahead, pull the pork, after all, Teresa told you to do it!

SERVES 8 **PREP TIME:** 30 minutes **COOK TIME:** 3 hours **TOTAL TIME:** 5 hours (includes 1 hour resting and 30 minutes cooling time)

FOR THE PORK

¼ cup (50 g) packed light brown sugar
2 tablespoons chili powder
1 teaspoon ground cumin
2 teaspoons kosher salt
1 teaspoon freshly ground black pepper
3½ pounds (1.5 kg) boneless pork shoulder
2 cups (480 ml) barbecue sauce, homemade (from I Don't Give a Rip Ribs with Ketchup, page 107) or store-bought

FOR THE SLAW

3 cups (690 g) packaged coleslaw mix
½ small red onion, thinly sliced
¾ cup (180 g) mayonnaise
1 teaspoon Dijon mustard

8 brioche buns, for serving
Potato chips, for serving

Amy's Note: If this isn't tasty, I give you permission to empty the contents of my handbag into a burning candle.

1. **PREPARE THE PORK:** In a bowl, stir together the brown sugar, chili powder, cumin, salt, and pepper. Pat the pork dry with paper towels. Rub the mixture all over the pork shoulder. Line an 18 × 14-inch (46 × 36 cm) baking sheet with parchment paper, add the seasoned pork, and let rest for 1 hour to come to room temperature.

2. When the pork has rested, preheat the oven to 325°F (170°C).

3. Transfer the pork to the oven and bake until the meat starts to pull away easily with a fork or reaches 200°F (90°C) on a meat thermometer, about 3 hours. Let rest for 30 minutes to cool.

4. Using your hands or two forks, pull that pork like a ponytail until it looks shredded. Combine with the barbecue sauce and mix well.

5. **MAKE THE SLAW:** In a large bowl, toss together the coleslaw mix, onion, mayo, and mustard and set aside.

6. To serve, place the bottom halves of the buns on plates, top with the pulled pork and then the slaw, then the other halves of the buns. Serve with potato chips.

Chef Stuart's Tip: A good shortcut is to buy your favorite bottled BBQ sauce. We all have our favorite. The pork can also be cooked in a pressure cooker to save you more time! Check the manufacturer's instructions for specific cooking times.

STAUB
STAUB

Women Soup-porting Women Manhattan Clam Chowder

Ramona has always had a strong constitution when it comes to supporting other women, so when Bethenny called and accused her of *not* doing just that, Ramona flipped it on "B" and told her that *she* actually doesn't support women. We love the drama of this Manhattan street corner phone fight, and we support women and their businesses. So ladies, after a long day at work, come home and warm up with this savory chowder. You deserve it. Just maybe don't have your boiling-hot soup during a boiling-hot argument . . . or your dog on a leash in the street, for that matter. This will take your taste buds on a "Ramonacoaster" of goodness.

SERVES 6 **PREP TIME:** 15 minutes **COOK TIME:** 45 minutes **TOTAL TIME:** 1 hour

---

- 2 dozen clams, such as littlenecks
- 2 tablespoons (30 g) unsalted butter
- 1 tablespoon olive oil
- 6 ounces (170 g) pancetta or bacon, diced
- 1 medium onion, diced
- 3 cloves garlic, chopped
- 2 stalks celery, diced
- 1 red bell pepper, diced
- 2 medium carrots, diced
- 2 Yukon Gold potatoes, cut into ½-inch (1.25 cm) cubes
- 1 teaspoon thyme leaves, chopped
- 1 (28 oz/800 g) can crushed San Marzano tomatoes
- 1 cup (240 ml) seafood stock or chicken stock
- ½ teaspoon red pepper flakes
- 1 teaspoon kosher salt
- ½ teaspoon freshly ground black pepper
- Chopped fresh parsley, for serving
- Oyster crackers, for serving

1. Bring a large pot of water to a boil. Add the clams and cook, covered, for 5 minutes. Drain the clams and let them cool. Discard any unopened clams. Remove the clam meat from the shells and set aside.

2. Empty and clean out the pot, then add the butter and oil and heat over medium heat until the butter is melted. Add the pancetta and cook until crispy, 5 to 7 minutes. Remove from the pan and set aside on a plate lined with paper towels.

3. Add the onion, garlic, celery, bell pepper, and carrots to the pot and cook until softened and lightly browned, 7 to 10 minutes. Add the potatoes, thyme, tomatoes, seafood stock, pepper flakes, salt, and black pepper. Bring to a boil, then reduce to a simmer and cook until the potatoes are fork-tender, 15 to 20 minutes. Stir in the clams.

4. Ladle the chowder into bowls, top with the pancetta and parsley. Serve immediately with oyster crackers.

Amy's Note: If you have the "or-dacity" to make this soup, please serve it to women only.

That's My OpinOnion Soup

Tamra has never held back from loudly expressing her opinion. One of our favorite reunion moments came when Tamra voiced her unfavorable opinion of Brooks and scream-yelled "That's my opinion!" We know Tamra has a tough exterior, but inside she has one of the most endearing personalities in the franchise. She has always been a superstar Housewife, and this is our superstar soup—a bold and aggressive top layer, with a sweet and savory layer of soup below. Let's just say our OpinOnion Soup comes in hot . . . like our esteemed and tenacious OC Housewife.

SERVES 4 **PREP TIME:** 10 minutes **COOK TIME:** 50 minutes **TOTAL TIME:** 1 hour

---

6 tablespoons (90 g) unsalted butter
2 tablespoons olive oil
2 medium onions, sliced
1 cup (240 ml) red wine
5 cups (1.1 liters) beef stock
1 tablespoon Worcestershire sauce
2 sprigs fresh thyme
1 teaspoon kosher salt
½ teaspoon freshly ground black pepper
2 slices sourdough bread, cut into cubes
2 cups (170 g) grated Gruyère cheese

Amy's Note: Like Tamra, baptize your taste buds with this heavenly soup.

1. In a large Dutch oven, melt the butter and oil over medium heat. Add the sliced onions and cook until they are softened and browned, 15 to 20 minutes. Add the wine and simmer for 3 to 5 more minutes.

2. Increase the heat to medium-high and add the beef stock, Worcestershire sauce, thyme, salt, and pepper. Simmer for 20 minutes over medium-low heat.

3. Position a rack in the center of the oven and preheat the broiler.

4. Ladle the soup into four 12-ounce (350 ml) ovenproof bowls and set them on a baking sheet. Dividing evenly among the bowls, place the bread cubes on top of the soup and sprinkle with the Gruyère cheese.

5. Broil until the cheese starts to melt and turn slightly brown, 2 to 3 minutes. Keep a close eye when doing this. Serve.

Chef Stuart's Tip: Just like you wouldn't leave the Housewives unattended at a reunion, do not step away from the soup when it is in the oven. The cheese can burn very quickly!

WHOLE PEELED
STAUB

When I Called You Garbage, I Meant You Were Garbage Soup

Did you know that "garbage" is an insult *and* a soup? The face-off between Caroline and Danielle helped us conjure up one of our most matchless and practical dishes. Danielle refused to back down from pressing charges against Ashley, which catapulted Caroline into an insult frenzy. But you don't have to call someone "a clown" or "garbage" to make this dish, and while you can just combine whatever is in your fridge for this soup, we do have suggestions based on our favorite vegetables! The perfect soup for a cold night spent thinking of ways to insult your enemies.

SERVES 6 TO 8 **PREP TIME:** 15 minutes **COOK TIME:** 45 minutes **TOTAL TIME:** 1 hour

---

1 tablespoon olive oil
6 slices bacon, roughly chopped
1 pound (450 g) ground beef (85% lean)
1 medium onion, diced
2 stalks celery, diced
2 carrots, diced
4 Yukon Gold potatoes, scrubbed and diced
1 (28 oz/800 g) can whole peeled San Marzano tomatoes, drained
1 teaspoon dried oregano
½ teaspoon dried basil
1 teaspoon kosher salt
½ teaspoon freshly ground black pepper
4 cups (960 ml) chicken stock
1 zucchini, diced
1 yellow squash, diced
Freshly grated parmesan cheese, for serving

1. In a large pot, heat the oil over medium-high heat. Add the bacon and cook until crisp. Remove from the pot and set aside.

2. In the same pot, over medium heat, cook the beef until cooked through, 7 to 10 minutes. Remove and set aside.

3. Add the onion, celery, and carrots to the pot and cook until softened, 4 to 5 minutes. Add the potatoes, tomatoes, oregano, basil, salt, pepper, chicken stock, and 3 cups (720 ml) water. Stir all the ingredients to combine. Bring to a boil, reduce the heat to medium-low, and simmer for 15 minutes. Stir in the zucchini, yellow squash, and cooked beef and let simmer for an additional 5 minutes.

4. Serve in bowls, topped with bacon bits and freshly grated parmesan.

Amy's Note: Let's put an end to all this nonsense and use our leftovers for garbage soup.

You Stole My Goddamn House Salad

Whether or not you believe Kyle *really* stole Kim's house, we know one thing for sure: Without their sisterly chemistry and drama, the Beverly Hills franchise wouldn't be the shining diamond that it is today. That fateful scene in the limo during the Season 1 finale proves that. Much like a starter salad is the foundation of any meal, Kim and Kyle are the foundation of the Beverly Hills Housewives. And many things have come between them, like Brandi, Kathy, and the infamous house. However, they inevitably let the drama bounce off their Birkins and move on. You can count on this salad as surely as you can count on Kim and Kyle, *always* bringing it to the table.

SERVES 4 TO 6 (DOUBLE THE RECIPE IF THE HILTON SISTERS ARE COMING OVER)

PREP TIME: 10 minutes **TOTAL TIME:** 20 minutes

---

2 heads butter lettuce
¼ cup (60 ml) L'Infinity Dress-ing (page 95)
1 tablespoon chopped fresh chives
1 tablespoon chopped fresh tarragon
1 tablespoon chopped fresh parsley
3 medium radishes, thinly sliced
½ cup (75 g) walnuts, chopped

Chef Stuart's Tip:
Don't be tempted to sub out the fresh herbs for dry here—in this case, fresh really makes a world of difference.

1. Tear off the large leaves from the stem of the butter lettuce, then break off the smaller leaves.

2. Arrange the leaves on plates or on a large platter starting with the larger leaves on the bottom and gradually working up to the smaller leaves on top.

3. Drizzle the dressing over the leaves, sprinkle with the fresh herbs, radish slices, and walnuts. Put on your pearl choker and serve in a stolen house.

Amy's Note: Home is where the heart is and my heart skips a beat every time the infamous house drama is brought up.

L'Infinity Dress-ing

When LeeAnne created the "L'Infinity Dress" we were blown away by the inventiveness of its use. She designed it to be worn in 175 ways! That must be a world record. Inspired by her one-of-a-kind dress, Chef Stuart created a dressing that you can use 175 different ways (in fact, many ways in this book). Just like LeeAnne's famous any-occasion dress, you can pair this dressing with any meal, for any occasion.

MAKES 2 CUPS **PREP TIME:** 5 minutes **TOTAL TIME:** 5 minutes

---

4 cloves garlic, smashed and peeled
5 jalapeño peppers, halved lengthwise and seeded
2 cups (40 g) cilantro, stems trimmed a bit but left on
¾ cup (210 g) Greek yogurt
¼ cup (60 ml) fresh lime juice
¼ cup (60 ml) red wine vinegar
½ teaspoon kosher salt
¼ cup (60 ml) extra-virgin olive oil
½ cup (120 ml) vegetable oil

Amy's Note: Sorry, D'Andra, you won't be able to make fun of this dressing, because it's perfect.

1. In a food processor, combine the garlic and jalapeños and pulse to loosely break them up. Add the cilantro and pulse a few times again.

2. Add the yogurt, lime juice, vinegar, and salt and blend. With the machine running, add each oil in a steady stream to emulsify everything.

3. Serve in one of 175 ways! This dressing will keep refrigerated for up to 5 days.

Chef Stuart's Tip: I like to use two different oils for this dressing. Extra-virgin has a stronger flavor than typical olive oil, so the mixture is nice in that you can grab some of that strong flavor without overpowering the dish. I especially like to use this dressing for tacos and as a dip with veggies, and you can even pair it with recipes throughout this book—get creative!

Beatless Brunch Beets and Burrata

We were giddy when former child star Kim Fields crossed over to reality TV and joined the Atlanta *Housewives* and challenged the ladies to a brunch without any makeup or glam. Although some Housewives did not abide by the au naturel rules (we're looking at you, Porsha, "beat" by the gods), some did, and they showed up in their rawest state, give or take some lashes and gloss. Similarly, these beets are gorgeous in their natural form—and this delicious app is as simple as a makeup-free face.

SERVES 4 TO 6 **PREP TIME:** 10 minutes **COOK TIME:** 1 hour (1 hour for a one-season Housewife)
TOTAL TIME: 1 hour 10 minutes

---

2 large red beets, trimmed
2 large yellow beets, trimmed
2 tablespoons extra-virgin olive oil
1 cup (120 g) walnuts
2 cups (40 g) arugula
8 ounces (225 g) burrata cheese
½ cup (120 ml) L'Infinity Dress-ing (page 95)
1 lemon, halved

Amy's Note: Glammed up or not, this app will always slay on your table.

1. Preheat the oven to 375°F (190°C).

2. Cut all of the beets in half lengthwise, root to stem. Place the red beets on a sheet of foil and place the yellow beets on another sheet of foil. Drizzle each group of beets with 1 tablespoon oil. Tightly wrap the beets in the foil and place on a baking sheet. Roast until fork-tender, 45 minutes to 1 hour. Let cool and peel.

3. Meanwhile, in a medium dry skillet, toast the walnuts over medium heat for 2 to 3 minutes, stirring constantly, until they become fragrant. Lightly chop. Set aside.

4. On a large platter, make a bed of arugula. Place the burrata in the center, then surround the burrata with the halved beets, alternating the colors. Drizzle with the dressing and sprinkle with the walnuts. Squeeze the juice from the lemon halves all over and serve. Enjoy!

Chef Stuart's Tip: Make sure to keep the beets separate while roasting, or the red beets will bleed into the yellow beets. Not quite as glam!

THIS ISN'T MY PLATE YOU STUPID FILET'N BITCH

PAGE 101

MEAT AND POULTRY

"I won't settle for anything less than being the main course."

We love a meaty, juicy storyline—remember the shuttle drama in Ireland among the entire OC cast? These main events have inspired the hearty mains you'll find here, like our Irish Bus Fight Stew (page 125), among many others. Now *these* are the dishes, and the drama, that we really love to chew on, right down to the bone.

This Isn't My Plate You Stupid Filet'n Bitch

Flying filets and hurling insults became the disquieting spectacle at The Quiet Woman. It began on a good note as Shannon ordered a delicious filet, but the scene hit a raucous crescendo when Shannon told Kelly to leave her table. Kelly roared at her to "Keep eating!" Shannon then threw a plate across the table and proclaimed the iconic line: "This isn't my plate, you stupid f-ing bitch!" We think this steak is pretty f-ing perfect—so good, in fact, that you'll be yelling, "This *is* my plate!" if anyone comes near it.

SERVES 4 **PREP TIME:** 15 minutes **COOK TIME:** 45 minutes **TOTAL TIME:** 1 hour, 45 minutes (includes 45 minutes resting time)

FOR THE STEAK

4 filet mignons (8 oz/225 g each), 2 inches (5 cm) thick
1 tablespoon olive oil
1 teaspoon kosher salt
½ teaspoon freshly ground black pepper

FOR THE RED WINE SAUCE

4 tablespoons olive oil
1 shallot, sliced
½ teaspoon freshly ground black pepper
2 cloves garlic, minced
2 sprigs fresh thyme
2½ tablespoons balsamic vinegar
1 cup (240 ml) red wine
1 cup (240 ml) beef stock
Kosher salt
2 tablespoons unsalted butter

1. Remove the steaks from the fridge and let them rest for 45 minutes to come to room temperature while you make the sauce.

2. **MAKE THE RED WINE SAUCE:** In a medium saucepan, heat the oil over medium-high heat and cook the shallot, 2 to 3 minutes.

3. Reduce the heat to medium, season with the pepper, and add the garlic and thyme. Continue cooking for 1 more minute, stirring often to prevent the shallot from burning.

4. Add the vinegar and cook until reduced to a syrup. Add the red wine and cook until reduced by two-thirds, 10 to 12 minutes.

5. Add the beef stock and bring to boil. Reduce the heat to low and simmer until the liquid is reduced by two-thirds again, about 10 minutes.

6. Add salt to taste and whisk in the butter. Set aside and keep warm.

7. **MAKE THE STEAK:** Preheat the oven to 375°F (190°C).

recipe continued on page 102

FOR SERVING

You Stole My Goddamn House Salad (page 93)
Forgotten Truffle Frois (page 33)

8. In a large cast-iron or other ovenproof skillet, heat the oil over medium-high heat. Season the steaks on both sides with the salt and pepper. When the oil begins to smoke, place the steaks in the skillet and cook for 3 to 4 minutes per side.

9. Transfer the skillet to the oven for 3 to 5 minutes, depending on how well-done you like your steak cooked (about 3 minutes for medium-rare).

10. Place the steaks on a cutting board and let rest for 5 minutes.

11. **TO SERVE**: Accompany the steaks with the red wine sauce, You Stole My Goddamn House Salad, and Truffle Frois.

Amy's Note: Enjoy your delectable steak, then promptly throw your plate across the table!

Vibrator Chicken Piccata

For those of you keeping score at home, the Season 12 RHONY Hamptons trip included three naked ladies in the pool, one absentee party host, some tiki torch throwing, and a vibrator in the chicken. Trashing Ramona's house never looked so fun! The episode is not for the faint of heart, but we're certain that this piccata dish is for everyone. Yes, you will need to serve the chicken on a beautiful platter and, alongside that . . . a vibrator.

SERVES 4 **PREP TIME:** 15 minutes **COOK TIME:** 15 minutes **TOTAL TIME:** 30 minutes

---

4 small boneless, skinless chicken breasts
⅓ cup (50 g) all-purpose flour
¼ cup (25 g) grated parmesan cheese
½ teaspoon onion powder
½ teaspoon garlic powder
¼ teaspoon freshly ground black pepper
4 tablespoons olive oil
6 tablespoons (90 g) unsalted butter
½ cup (120 ml) dry white wine
Juice of 1 lemon
½ cup (60 g) capers, drained
¼ cup (15 g) chopped fresh parsley
You Stole My Goddamn House Salad (page 93), for serving

1. Preheat the oven to 200°F (90°C).

2. To butterfly the chicken, slice the chicken breasts horizontally. Place each butterflied breast between two pieces of plastic wrap and pound them with the smooth side of a meat pounder to a ½ inch (12 mm) thickness.

3. In a shallow bowl, whisk together the flour, parmesan, onion powder, garlic powder, and pepper. Dredge the chicken cutlets in the flour mixture and set aside.

In a large skillet, heat 2 tablespoons of the oil and 2 tablespoons of the butter over medium heat. Add two of the chicken cutlets and cook for about 3 minutes per side. Repeat with the remaining chicken, oil, and 2 tablespoons of the butter. Place the cooked chicken on an 18 × 14-inch (46 cm × 36 cm) baking sheet and place in the oven to keep warm.

4. Over medium heat, pour the wine, lemon juice, and capers into the skillet, scraping up any browned bits. Cook until the sauce reduces by half. Remove from the heat and stir in the remaining 2 tablespoons butter and the parsley.

5. Remove the chicken from the oven and place a cutlet in the center of each plate. Drizzle with the sauce. Add a vibrator for a joke. Serve with You Stole My Goddamn House Salad.

Coke-Marinated Kebabs in the Bathroom

Timing is everything, and the time was now for Rinna to play tit for tat with Dorit in retaliation for the Xanax accusations of the previous year (see Banana Xanax Smoothie, page 19). Rinna asked Dorit if she was doing coke in the bathroom at her party, leaving everyone stunned with mouths agape. Because the ladies were at a dinner in Hong Kong, we captured the Asian influence in these kebabs while also using coke . . . well, not the real "coke." When you're finished eating this, just remember, if you get up from the table to go get "touched up," then you might get a little heat from your dinner guests. This dish is not a "low blow," by the way. Oh, and if it's too hot, "blow" on it. Just don't "blow" off this dish, it's amazing! Okay, I'm done with the blow jokes . . . enjoy!

SERVES 4 **PREP TIME:** 10 minutes **COOK TIME:** 15 minutes **TOTAL TIME:** 2 hours 25 minutes (includes 2 hours marinating time)

FOR THE MARINATED BEEF

1 cup (240 ml) Coca-Cola
½ cup (120 ml) soy sauce
¼ cup (60 ml) hoisin sauce
¼ cup (60 ml) fresh lemon juice
⅓ cup (80 ml) olive oil
¼ cup (60 ml) Worcestershire sauce
4 cloves garlic, minced
2½ pounds (1135 g) rib-eye steaks, cut into 2-inch (5 cm) cubes

FOR THE KEBABS

Eight 10-inch (25 cm) wooden skewers
2 red bell peppers, cut into 2-inch (5 cm) pieces
2 yellow bell peppers, cut into 2-inch (5 cm) pieces

Amy's Note: You don't know what I go through at night, so I need you guys to make this dish.

1. **MARINATE THE BEEF:** In a gallon-size zip-top plastic bag, combine the cola, soy sauce, hoisin, lemon juice, oil, Worcestershire sauce, and garlic. Add the meat and marinate in the fridge for 2 hours or even overnight.

2. **ASSEMBLE THE KEBABS:** Place 3 pieces of meat on each of the skewers, alternating with yellow and red bell pepper pieces in between the pieces of meat.

3. Preheat a grill to medium-high (or preheat a grill pan until piping hot). Add the skewers to the grill grates (or pan) and cook meat 2 to 4 minutes per side (4 minutes will be well-done). Let sit for 3 minutes before serving.

4. Eat in the bathroom.

Chef Stuart's Tip: Soak the wooden skewers in water for at least 1 hour before cooking to prevent them from burning on the grill!

KETCHUP

I Don't Give a Rip Ribs

WITH KETCHUP

Sometimes it's the mothers of the Housewives that become the breakout stars, and this Dallas spitfire mom is not just a Texas star, but a shooting star in our book. D'Andra's mother, Momma Dee, taught us that the way to a man's heart is through his stomach. We're happy to say that these ribs are a surefire way to get that man—or any man, really. So here is our version of Momma Dee–inspired sweet and spicy ribs, perfect for any summer backyard cookout. And, yes, of course we used a *lot* of ketchup to create this one. These ribs are so good, you'll want to change your name to Simmons.

SERVES 4 TO 6 **PREP TIME:** 15 minutes **COOK TIME:** 2 hours 40 minutes
TOTAL TIME: 3 hours 10 minutes

- 2 racks baby back ribs (each 3 to 3½ lb/1.3 to 1.5 kg)
- Kosher salt and freshly ground black pepper
- 2 tablespoons olive oil

FOR THE BBQ SAUCE

- 2 cups (470 g) ketchup
- ¼ cup (60 ml) apple cider vinegar
- ¼ cup (60 ml) dark molasses
- 2 tablespoons Worcestershire sauce
- ½ cup (100 g) packed light brown sugar
- 2 teaspoons Dijon mustard
- ½ teaspoon garlic powder
- ½ teaspoon onion powder
- ½ teaspoon kosher salt
- ¼ teaspoon freshly ground black pepper

1. Preheat the oven to 350°F (175°C).

2. Place each rack of ribs on a sheet of foil, season them with salt and pepper, and rub the oil all over them. Wrap with another sheet of foil and place the wrapped ribs on a rimmed baking sheet. Bake until a fork easily pulls the meat from the bone, 2 to 2½ hours.

3. **MEANWHILE, MAKE THE BBQ SAUCE:** In a saucepan, combine all the ingredients and simmer over low heat, stirring often, for 8 to 10 minutes to marry the flavors and thicken the sauce.

4. Remove the ribs from the oven, uncover, and brush the BBQ sauce all over the ribs. Return to the oven for 15 minutes. Baste with the sauce again and bake for 15 minutes longer. Remove from the oven.

5. Turn on the broiler. Brush more sauce on the ribs and broil until they become crisp and charred, 2 to 3 minutes. Serve with any leftover sauce on the side and grab some napkins.

Amy's Note: Hand the keys to your business to your heir and retire with this down-home dish.

Chef Stuart's Tip: Put the ribs in the oven for the amount of time that Momma Dee was retired (not long). But seriously, when broiling, do not walk away from the oven; the sauce is sugary so it can burn pretty fast!

COTO DE CASSEROLE
PAGE 109

Coto de Casserole

We're giving Vicki the casserole that she never got. When Brooks endured his ailment, all Vicki wanted from her friends was a little comfort, empathy, and a casserole—and maybe for them not to ask any questions. Instead, she was met with skepticism, contention, and a Housewife detective named Meghan who tried to expose the truth. Turned out that Brooks was too chicken to tell the truth about his alleged cancer, and it's now known as the infamous cancer scam. Perfect to make for a friend in need or a family dinner.

SERVES 8 **PREP TIME:** 15 minutes **COOK TIME:** 30 minutes **TOTAL TIME:** 45 minutes

Kosher salt
10 ounces (125 g) penne pasta
1 teaspoon olive oil
4 tablespoons (60 g) unsalted butter
1 large carrot, diced
2 stalks celery, diced
1 medium onion, diced
4 cloves garlic, minced
½ pound (230 g) button mushrooms, sliced
1 tablespoon all-purpose flour
1½ cups (360 ml) heavy cream
Cooking spray
1 (28 oz/800 g) can diced San Marzano tomatoes, drained
3 cups (420 g) shredded rotisserie chicken
8 ounces (225 g) shredded sharp cheddar cheese
½ cup (45 g) grated parmesan cheese

1. Preheat the oven to 375°F (190°C).
2. Bring a large pot of salted water to a boil. Add the pasta and cook according to the package directions, less 1 minute for al dente. Drain, return to the pot, and toss with the oil. Set aside to cool.
3. In a large skillet, melt the butter over medium heat. Add the carrot, celery, onion, garlic, and mushrooms and cook until the vegetables are softened, 7 to 10 minutes.
4. Sprinkle in the flour and stir for 30 seconds to combine. Stir in the cream and simmer until thickened, about 3 minutes. Season with 1 teaspoon salt and stir in the cooled pasta until well coated.
5. Mist a 13 × 9-inch (33 × 23 cm) deep baking dish with cooking spray. Spread the diced tomatoes over the bottom of the dish. Add the rotisserie chicken and then the pasta mixture. Top with the cheddar and parmesan cheese.
6. Bake until the cheese is bubbling and starting to turn brown, about 20 minutes. Let sit for 2 to 3 minutes before serving.

Amy's Note: I've never conned anyone! The truth is that this casserole is delightful.

Soapy Lemon Chicken à la Adrienne

Perhaps a pandemic didn't need to exist for Adrienne to wash her food; after all, she was on the ground floor for sanitizing comestibles. A chef she is not (hence why she had her private Chef Bernie), so the time came when Lisa Vanderpump took her under her (chicken) wing and gave her a cooking lesson. When LVP instructed her to wash the chicken, Adrienne began to wash the chicken in the sink with dish soap! LVP stood aghast and appalled in her pink platform pumps. So, to give you that same vibe without washing out your mouth, we are going to combine the flavor of tarragon with some lemon for a crisp, clean flavor.

SERVES 4 **PREP TIME:** 20 minutes **COOK TIME:** 1 hour 30 minutes **TOTAL TIME:** 2 hours 5 minutes (includes 15 minutes resting time)

---

1 whole roasting chicken (5 to 6 lb/2.5 to 2.7 kg)
Kosher salt and freshly ground black pepper
1 medium onion, quartered
1 lemon, cut into 4 wedges
1 head garlic, halved horizontally
4 sprigs fresh tarragon
4 sprigs fresh thyme
3 large carrots, cut into 3-inch (8 cm) chunks
2 bulbs fennel, quartered
2 tablespoons olive oil
1 stick (4 oz/115 g) unsalted butter, melted
1 cup (240 ml) chicken stock
Mashed potatoes and steamed green beans, for serving

Amy's Note: If you're one of those people who thinks tarragon tastes like soap, well, lucky you—you're getting the authentic Adrienne experience.

1. Preheat the oven to 425°F (220°C).

2. Pat the chicken inside and out with paper towels (don't wash with water and soap, don't be like Adrienne!). Season generously inside and out with salt and pepper. Stuff the cavity with the onion quarters, 3 lemon wedges, half of the garlic, the tarragon, and thyme. Again, no soap!

3. Drop the carrots, fennel, remaining lemon wedges, and the other half of the garlic head into a roasting pan. Drizzle with the oil, season with some salt and pepper, and toss to coat. Arrange the vegetables toward the center of the pan.

4. Tie the chicken legs together with kitchen string and tuck the wing tips under the body of the chicken. Brush with the melted butter all over. Place on top of the vegetables and add the chicken stock to the pan.

5. Place in the center of the oven and roast until the juices run clear and the breast registers 160°F (75°C) on a thermometer, about 1 hour 30 minutes.

6. Let the chicken rest for 15 minutes to let all those juices come together before carving. Serve with some mashed potatoes and steamed green beans.

Chef Stuart's Tip: A "roasting" chicken refers to a chicken less than 8 months old, weighing between 4 to 6 pounds. This dish pairs wonderfully with the L'Infinity Dress-ing (page 95).

Bangin' Meditation Bowl Chicken Paillard

We hit the flavor gong with this dish! Shannon and Kelly's friendship has had its ups and downs, and this incident was the straw that broke the camel's back—okay, maybe it was the bowl that gonged the camel's head. Kelly took it too far at the wellness retreat when she turned Shannon's sound bath into a bloodbath by pulling a prank. Instead of banging on a bowl with your friend's head in it, bang on this chicken and make a gorgeous, tasty chicken dish. For extra points, serve in a meditation bowl. CAT scan not included.

 **SERVES 2** **PREP TIME:** 20 minutes **COOK TIME:** 15 minutes **TOTAL TIME:** 35 minutes

---

2 small boneless, skinless chicken breasts
Kosher salt and freshly ground black pepper
3 tablespoons olive oil
2 cups (40 g) arugula
1 shallot, thinly sliced
¼ cup (20 g) sliced almonds, toasted
1 tablespoon red wine vinegar
2 medium tomatoes, diced
1 tablespoon balsamic vinegar
Juice of ½ lemon
½ teaspoon flaky sea salt
Lemon wedges, for serving

1. To butterfly the chicken, slice the chicken breasts horizontally. Place each butterflied breast between two pieces of plastic wrap and pound them with the smooth side of a meat pounder to a ½-inch (12 mm) thickness. Season with salt and pepper.

2. In a large nonstick skillet, heat 1 tablespoon of the oil over medium-high heat until you see it slightly smoke. Set one of the chicken cutlets in the pan away from you to prevent splattering and cook for 4 minutes per side. Repeat with the second chicken cutlet and another 1 tablespoon oil.

3. Meanwhile, in a bowl, toss together the arugula, shallot, almonds, red wine vinegar, and remaining 1 tablespoon oil. Set aside.

4. In a small bowl, toss together the tomatoes, balsamic, lemon juice, and sea salt.

5. Place the chicken cutlets in the centers of 2 plates and top with the arugula salad and tomato salad. Serve with lemon wedges.

6. Meditate for 5 minutes, then enjoy.

TICKET
336022
TICKET
336021
INDIANA TICKET CO.
TICKET
336031
TICKET
336030
TICKET
336029
TICKET
336028
INDIANA TICKET CO.
TICKET
336037
TICKET
INDIANA TICKET CO.
TICKET
336044
TICKET
336045
TICKET

Chili con Carney

We made this Texas dish "carney-style" in honor of LeeAnne. She has always been transparent about her tumultuous upbringing in the carnival. "Be real careful," this dish is spicy and reflects her hot temper. Known to throw a glass or two and speak her mind, she never shied away from sharing her life. This chili is ideal for family dinner after a night out at the carnival. Like Tiffany "takes up" for LeeAnne, we take up for this meal every f'ing time.

SERVES 8 TO 10 **PREP TIME:** 20 minutes **COOK TIME:** 40 minutes **TOTAL TIME:** 1 hour

4 tablespoons olive oil
2 pounds (910 g) ground beef (85% lean)
2 medium onions, diced
2 tablespoons tomato paste
4 cloves garlic, minced
1 red bell pepper, diced
1 green bell pepper, diced
1 tablespoon chili powder
1 teaspoon ground cumin
1 teaspoon kosher salt
½ teaspoon freshly ground black pepper
1 (28 oz/800 g) can diced San Marzano tomatoes, drained
4 cups (960 ml) beef stock
1 cup (250 g) canned kidney beans, drained and rinsed
1 cup (250 g) canned black beans, drained and rinsed

FOR SERVING

1 cup (240 g) sour cream
1 avocado, diced
1 cup (85 g) shredded Mexican cheese blend
1 jalapeño, sliced
Cilantro leaves

1. In a Dutch oven or a large pot, heat 2 tablespoons of the oil over medium-high heat. Add the beef and cook until browned, 8 to 10 minutes. Remove and set aside.

2. Add the remaining 2 tablespoons oil and the onions to the same pot and cook until beginning to brown, about 5 minutes. Add the tomato paste and cook for 1 minute. Stir in the garlic, bell peppers, chili powder, cumin, salt, and black pepper.

3. Return the cooked beef to the pot along with the diced tomatoes and beef stock. Bring to a boil, then reduce to a simmer and cook, uncovered, for 20 to 25 minutes to allow the flavors to come together.

4. Add the beans and cook for another 5 to 6 minutes to heat through. Serve with dollops of the sour cream, the avocado, Mexican cheese blend, jalapeño slices, and cilantro leaves.

Amy's Note: It's so good, you'll punch a trolley!

Gorga-zola Balls

Joe Gorga has guts, gusto, and, dare we say . . . balls. After his triumphant arrival onto the New Jersey *Housewives* when he slammed on a table and cried to his father at little Joey's christening, we knew we could never quit him. He carries the weight of a lot of family drama and isn't afraid to put it all out there. He can get a little cheesy and a lot ballsy, so we give you Gorga-zola Balls! These provide a delicious twist to the traditional meatball with some added Gorgonzola cheesiness. If Joe were to suggest anything, it would be that you eat these twice a day to "get the poison out."

MAKES 16 TO 18 MEATBALLS (TO SERVE 6) **PREP TIME:** 20 minutes **COOK TIME:** 20 minutes **TOTAL TIME:** 40 minutes

---

Cooking spray
1 pound (450 g) ground pork
1 pound (450 g) ground beef (85% lean)
1 teaspoon kosher salt
½ teaspoon freshly ground black pepper
4 cloves garlic, minced
2 large eggs, beaten
¾ cup (70 g) grated parmesan cheese
1 cup (110 g) Italian-style fine dried bread crumbs
6 ounces (170 g) crumbled Gorgonzola cheese
2 tablespoons olive oil
3 cups Thick as Thieves Sauce (page 155)

1. Preheat the oven to 400°F (200°C). Mist an 18 × 14-inch (46 × 36 cm) baking sheet with cooking spray.

2. Place the meat in a large bowl. Add the salt, pepper, garlic, eggs, parmesan, and bread crumbs. Using your hands mix and combine well.

3. Using a 2-inch (5 cm) ice cream scoop, scoop out meat into your hands and roll lightly into balls. Make an indentation and add ½ teaspoon blue cheese to the center. Pull the meat over the cheese and re-form into a ball. Place on the prepared baking sheet. Repeat until all the meat is used up.

4. In a large nonstick skillet, heat the oil over medium-high heat. Add the meatballs and brown, 2 minutes on each side. Return the meatballs to the baking sheet.

5. Place the baking sheet in the oven and bake until cooked through, 8 to 10 minutes. Serve with the Thick as Thieves Sauce.

Chef Stuart's Tip: These balls are also perfect for appetizers, just toss the Gorgonzola cheese into the beef mixture and roll into 1-inch balls.

Scary Island Skirt Steak in Jill Zarin-ade

It wasn't all Turtle Time on this trip! A girls' getaway to the Virgin Islands for Ramona's vow renewal turned into one of the most fantastically bizarre and unbelievable episodes ever. Kelly's breakdown drove the madness into high gear with her strange references to satchels of gold, kabuki, murder accusations, and Al Sharpton. While the ladies did the best they could to de-escalate the odd behavior, they were done with Kelly's craziness. Then, Jill's surprise visit threw things into another tailspin when her arrival caused them all to lose it during mani/pedis, and Ramona asked Jill to leave. What an ordeal! This skirt steak recipe competes with Bethenny's steak dinner on this trip—and rest assured, Stuart is a "Chef," not a "cook," so you will love this, no strings attached.

SERVES 4 TO 6 **PREP TIME:** 10 minutes **COOK TIME:** 20 minutes **TOTAL TIME:** 50 minutes (includes 20 minutes marinating time)

1½ pounds (680 g) skirt steak, sinews and membrane removed, fat trimmed (ask your butcher to do this!)
½ cup (120 ml) reduced-sodium soy sauce
½ cup (120 ml) port
½ cup (120 ml) balsamic vinegar
½ teaspoon red pepper flakes
3 scallions, sliced, for garnish
Sesame seeds, for garnish
You Stole My Goddamn House Salad (page 93), for serving

Amy's Note: This is a mouthwatering dish that will make you "zip it."

1. In a gallon-size zip-top plastic bag, combine the steak, soy sauce, port, vinegar, and pepper flakes. Marinate, or rather, Zarin-ate, for at least 20 minutes.

2. Preheat a grill to medium-high (or heat up a cast-iron skillet until piping hot).

3. Meanwhile, remove the steak from the bag and pour the marinade into a small saucepan. Reduce the marinade over medium-high heat for 5 to 10 minutes to thicken.

4. Pat the steak with paper towels to remove excess marinade. Place the steak on the grill (or skillet) and cook for 3 minutes per side. Set aside on a plate under tented foil and let rest for 5 minutes.

5. Slice the steak against the grain into ½-inch (1.25 cm) slices. Drizzle with the reduced marinade and sprinkle with the scallions and sesame seeds.

6. Serve with You Stole My Goddamn House Salad.

On-Time Teddi Turkey Tacos

We've all been there . . . sitting alone in a public place waiting anxiously for our "late" friend to arrive, sipping on wine. And Dorit took it to the next level by making the Accountability Coach herself, Teddi, wait 48 minutes—yes, *exactly* 48 minutes. Not the person you want to keep waiting. Well, we won't keep you waiting long for this dish because it is the perfect, fast, go-to meal that you can whip up at a moment's notice. Great for family dinner or before those long overseas calls with your swimwear company.

SERVES 4 **PREP TIME:** 5 minutes **COOK TIME:** 15 minutes **TOTAL TIME:** 20 minutes

---

1 tablespoon olive oil
1 pound (450 g) ground turkey
1 tablespoon chili powder
1 tablespoon ground cumin
½ teaspoon paprika
1 teaspoon garlic powder
1 teaspoon onion powder
1 teaspoon kosher salt
8 corn tortillas

FOR THE TOPPINGS

Sour cream
Diced avocado
Cilantro leaves
Sliced red Fresno chile
Shredded Mexican cheese blend

Amy's Note: If these aren't the tastiest turkey tacos you've ever had, you can hold me accountable.

1. In a large skillet, heat the oil over medium-high heat. Add the turkey and cook until it begins to brown, 6 to 8 minutes.

2. Meanwhile, in a small bowl, mix together the chili powder, cumin, paprika, garlic powder, onion powder, and salt.

3. Add the spice mixture to the turkey, stir to coat, and continue cooking until the liquid is absorbed, 3 to 5 minutes.

4. Cover the tortillas with a damp paper towel and warm them in the microwave for 20 to 30 seconds.

5. Assemble the tacos with the turkey mixture and your favorite toppings and just make sure your friends are on time.

Chef Stuart's Tip: The seasoning in this recipe can work with other proteins so give it a try! I love this zesty blend with shrimp.

Gone with the Wind Fricassee

It seemed like most of Anguilla heard Kenya and Porsha's epic poolside shouting match, so gloriously cinematic it inspired Kenya to dub herself "Gone with the Wind fabulous" before twirling off to her hotel room (and later recording a song called, well, "Gone with the Wind Fabulous"). But really, this Kenya/Porsha fight was simmering for ages, long before the ladies touched down in the Caribbean. This slow-burn brawl naturally got us thinking about braises, and what is a fricassee if not a delicious way to slowly cook meat until tender? While this feud is probably about as tender as a bruise for Kenya and Porsha, we can promise you this fricassee is *fabulously*, fall-off-the-bone tender.

SERVES 4 **PREP TIME:** 30 minutes **COOK TIME:** 1 hour **TOTAL TIME:** 1 hour 30 minutes

---

4 bone-in, skin-on chicken thighs
4 chicken drumsticks
1½ teaspoons kosher salt
1 teaspoon freshly ground black pepper
4 tablespoons (60 g) unsalted butter
2 tablespoons olive oil
1 medium onion, diced
2 medium carrots, diced
2 stalks celery, diced
3 cloves garlic, roughly chopped
10 ounces (160 g) button mushrooms, quartered
2 tablespoons all-purpose flour
1 cup (240 ml) dry white wine
3 cups (720 ml) chicken stock
3 sprigs fresh thyme
3 large egg yolks, at room temperature
⅓ cup (80 ml) heavy cream
3 tablespoons chopped fresh tarragon
Mashed potatoes, for serving

1. Season the chicken with the salt and pepper. In a large Dutch oven, heat 2 tablespoons of the butter and 1 tablespoon of the oil over medium heat. Add 2 chicken thighs and 2 chicken drumsticks to the Dutch oven to brown on all sides, 8 to 10 minutes. Transfer the chicken to a plate. Wipe out the Dutch oven and repeat with the remaining butter, oil, and 4 pieces chicken. Set all the chicken aside.

2. Add the onion, carrots, and celery to the Dutch oven and cook until the vegetables are softened, 5 to 6 minutes. Add the garlic and mushrooms and cook until all the liquid from the mushrooms has evaporated, another 5 to 6 minutes.

3. Sprinkle in the flour and stir for 20 seconds to combine. Increase the heat to medium-high, add the wine, and stir until the mixture has thickened, 1 to 2 minutes. Stir in the stock and thyme.

4. Return the chicken to the Dutch oven, placing it on top of the vegetables and liquid. Partially cover the Dutch oven to let steam escape, bring to a simmer over medium-low heat, and cook until the chicken's juices run clear, 10 to 15 minutes. Remove the chicken to an 18 × 14-inch (46 × 36 cm) sheet pan and cover with foil to keep warm.

Chef Stuart's Tip:

This recipe is a bit more of a process than most in this book. It is so worth it. My tip is to read the recipe three times before you start to cook it and twirl three times after you cook it!

5. In a medium bowl, whisk together the egg yolks, cream, and 2 tablespoons of the tarragon. Scoop about ½ cup of the cooking liquid from the Dutch oven and, whisking constantly, slowly add to the egg yolk mixture. This process tempers the eggs so they don't scramble. Stir the warmed egg mixture into the Dutch oven.

6. Return the chicken to the Dutch oven. Bring to a light simmer and cook for 2 to 3 minutes. Serve sprinkled with the remaining 1 tablespoon tarragon and some mashed potatoes on the side—we hear starchy carbohydrates are good for wound healing.

Amy's Note: Twirl this dish out flawlessly for your frenemies.

Wig Snatcciatore

This dish is not as mysterious as what's under Kim's wig—it's our hot take on chicken cacciatore. There's nothing like following a nice meal with a street-side argument. Take your inspiration from the wig snatch heard 'round the world. This dish perfectly sums up the heated fight in Atlanta when Shereé dared to "tug" Kim's wig. Much like that moment, this dish is peppered and spicy—enough so that it will keep you on your toes if anyone tries to shift your wig during dinner.

SERVES 4 **PREP TIME:** 15 minutes **COOK TIME:** 45 minutes **TOTAL TIME:** 1 hour

---

¾ cup (100 g) all-purpose flour
2 teaspoons kosher salt
1 teaspoon freshly ground black pepper
8 boneless, skinless chicken thighs
4 tablespoons olive oil
1 medium onion, diced
3 cloves garlic, chopped
1 red bell pepper, sliced
2 tablespoons tomato paste
½ cup (120 ml) red wine, such as Pinot Noir
1 (28 oz/800 g) can whole peeled San Marzano tomatoes, drained
¾ cup (180 ml) chicken stock
½ cup (60 g) capers, drained
2 teaspoons dried oregano
10 fresh basil leaves, chopped
Cooked angel hair pasta, for serving

Chef Stuart's Tip:
Chicken thighs are used in this dish because they will not dry out. If there are any leftovers, the flavors are even better the next day!

1. In a gallon-size zip-top plastic bag, combine the flour, salt, and pepper. Add 4 of the chicken thighs and toss to coat the chicken. Remove and place on a plate. Add the remaining 4 thighs to the bag and toss to coat.

2. In a large nonstick skillet, heat 2 tablespoons of the oil over medium-high heat. Add 4 pieces of chicken and brown all over, 3 minutes per side. Remove the chicken and set aside. Repeat with the remaining 2 tablespoons of oil and 4 pieces of chicken.

3. Reduce the heat to medium. Add the onion, garlic, and bell pepper and cook until tender, 3 to 5 minutes. Stir in the tomato paste and cook for another 1 to 2 minutes. Add the wine and cook for 2 minutes, scraping any browned bits from the bottom of the pan.

4. Stir in the tomatoes and break them up using a wooden spoon or potato masher.

5. Add the chicken stock and bring to a simmer. Stir in the capers and oregano.

6. Add the chicken thighs to the sauce and simmer over medium-low heat until cooked through and the sauce thickens, 10 to 12 minutes. Transfer the chicken to a platter and cover with foil to keep warm.

7. Simmer the sauce for 2 to 4 minutes to thicken. Spoon the sauce over the chicken and sprinkle with the chopped basil. Serve with angel hair pasta.

Amy's Note: This chicken dish is so savory and delicious your friends (and enemies) will definitely try to snatch this one away.

Irish Bus Fight Stew

It was a six-Housewife pileup inside a bus in Ireland at 3 a.m.—it was dark, but the altercation was even darker. Some might remember the iconic scene as a gang-up on Kelly, while others may say it was when Vicki betrayed Shannon, or perhaps that both Shannon and Tamra turned on Vicki. After rumors and insults were hurled across the bus, the "stew" hit the fan. There are lots of ingredients in this authentic Irish stew because there were lots of layers to this group fight.

SERVES 4 **PREP TIME:** 10 minutes **COOK TIME:** 30 minutes **TOTAL TIME:** 40 minutes

---

3 tablespoons olive oil
2 pounds (900 g) sirloin steak, cut into 2-inch (5 cm) cubes
1 teaspoon kosher salt
1 teaspoon freshly ground black pepper
1 medium onion, roughly sliced
4 cloves garlic, roughly chopped
3 carrots, cut into rounds ½ inch (1.25 cm) thick
2 cups (250 g) button mushrooms, halved
¾ cup (180 ml) dry red wine, such as Cabernet
1 (15 oz/450 g) can cannellini beans, drained and rinsed
1 (28 oz/800 g) can diced San Marzano tomatoes
1 tablespoon chopped fresh chives

1. In a large skillet or Dutch oven, heat 2 tablespoons of the oil over medium-high heat. Season the meat with the salt and pepper. Working in small batches, add the beef to the pan and sear on all sides. This will take roughly 10 to 15 minutes total. Remove the meat and set aside.

2. Reduce the heat to medium, add the onion and garlic, and stir for 3 minutes to soften. Add the carrots and cook for another 2 minutes. Add the mushrooms and cook for 3 to 4 minutes.

3. Increase the heat to high, add the wine, and scrape any browned bits from the bottom of the pan. Reduce the heat to medium and simmer for 2 to 3 minutes.

4. Add the cannellini beans and tomatoes, and simmer for 2 to 3 minutes. Stir in the seared beef and any accumulated juices and simmer for 2 more minutes.

5. Serve sprinkled with the chives.

Chef Stuart's Tip: I've lightened up this stew by subbing out potatoes for beans, but if you want to go traditional, leave out the beans and add steamed, diced potatoes.

Amy's Note: Do your best Shannon-inspired Irish accent and don your green sequins to make this stew. Top o' the mornin' to ya!

KYLE BY ALENE TUNA
PAGE 129

SEAFOOD

"I don't deal with tilapia, or any other bottom feeders."

When it comes to seafood, we truly "sea each otha." Because once you crack through that crustacean shell of pride and ego, you get to that rare delicacy that is a vulnerable Housewife. Maybe it's that special bonding over sushi or salmon (with a glass or four of Sauvy B) that we see so often with the Housewives that has them going for fish, hook, line, and sinker. (Hey, we're not kidding—one Housewife even has a whole room dedicated to fish, which is why we give you Fish Room Cioppino, page 139.) So dive in—these recipes are a catch!

Kyle by Alene Tuna

Kyle's passion for designer brands and luxury fashion came to fruition when she opened a boutique on a hot-spot street in Beverly Hills. Racks of Kyle-inspired clothes were draped from wall to wall, from caftans to wide-brim hats, dangly earrings, and drapey blouses. Kyle's collaboration with Alene was one that kept fans intrigued, including us, and we're still obsessed with her luxury lifestyle. Frankly, we can't think of a dish more raw or chic than tuna tartare. This dish is as petite as Kyle, and best of all, the prep is simple and sophisticated. You won't say "goodbye Kyle" to this recipe, you'll say hello!

SERVES 4 **PREP TIME:** 30 minutes **TOTAL TIME:** 30 minutes

---

FOR THE TUNA TARTARE

2 ahi tuna steaks (5 oz/125 g each), cut into ½-inch (1.25 cm) cubes
½ English cucumber, peeled and cut into small dice
2 cups (40 g) arugula
3 scallions, thinly sliced
2 teaspoons chopped fresh cilantro
¼ cup (35 g) toasted sesame seeds
½ teaspoon sriracha sauce
¼ teaspoon kosher salt
¼ teaspoon freshly ground black pepper
Juice of 1 lime
1 avocado, diced

FOR THE DRESSING

1 scallion, light-green part only, thinly sliced
1 tablespoon grated fresh ginger
1 clove garlic, minced
2 tablespoons soy sauce
1 tablespoon rice vinegar
1 tablespoon sesame oil

FOR SERVING

Toasted sesame seeds
1 scallion, light-green part only, thinly sliced
Tortilla chips

1. Place four martini glasses in the fridge.

2. **MAKE THE TUNA TARTARE:** In a large bowl, combine the tuna, cucumber, arugula, scallions, cilantro, sesame seeds, sriracha, salt, pepper, and lime juice and mix well until combined. Add the avocado and toss gently to combine.

3. **MAKE THE DRESSING:** In a small bowl, whisk together the scallions, ginger, garlic, soy sauce, vinegar, and sesame oil. Add the dressing to the tuna tartare and stir to combine.

4. **TO SERVE:** Remove the glasses from the fridge and scoop the tartare into them. Top with some sesame seeds and the chopped scallions. Serve with tortilla chips.

Chef Stuart's Tip: This is my go-to tuna tartare recipe. It can be made year-round, but it's such a hit to serve in the warmer months of spring and summer.

Amy's Note: Just be honest . . . admit that you love tuna. Slip into your caftan and get into a Beverly Hills state of mind with this exquisite dish.

recipe photo on page 126

Oysters Ramona-feller

It's no secret that Ramona is "ageless," *and* that she loves her oysters. So we give you an oyster recipe reimagined for her lust for this shelled delicacy. If you're feeling "frisqué," make a dozen of these oysters and double-book yourself with dates. These can serve as the perfect aphrodisiac or as a fabulous app at a lunch for fifty of your closest girlfriends (just double the recipe).

MAKES 24 OYSTERS **PREP TIME:** 15 minutes **COOK TIME:** 15 minutes **TOTAL TIME:** 30 minutes

---

5 tablespoons (75 g) unsalted butter
1 medium onion, finely chopped
3 cloves garlic, minced
12 ounces (45 g) fresh spinach, chopped
1 cup (90 g) grated parmesan cheese
1 cup (110 g) fine dried bread crumbs
1 tablespoon fresh lemon juice
1 tablespoon chopped fresh parsley
¼ teaspoon freshly ground black pepper
1½ pounds (625 g) kosher salt
2 dozen fresh oysters in the shell, washed and shucked, bottom shells reserved

1. Preheat the oven to 425°F (220°C).

2. In a large skillet, melt the butter over medium heat. Add the onion and cook until softened, 5 to 6 minutes. Add the garlic and spinach and cook until the spinach has wilted, 2 to 3 minutes. Remove from the heat and stir in the parmesan, bread crumbs, lemon juice, parsley, and pepper until well combined.

3. Spread 1 pound (450 g) kosher salt onto an 18 × 14-inch (46 × 36 cm) sheet pan.

4. Lightly press the bottom oyster shells down into the salt. Place an oyster into each shell. Top each oyster with about 1½ tablespoons of the spinach/bread crumb mixture.

5. Transfer to the oven and bake until golden, 8 to 10 minutes. Meanwhile, pour the remaining kosher salt onto a serving platter. Place the cooked oysters on top, and serve immediately.

Chef Stuart's Tip: Buy the oysters the day you are going to use them. If you don't want to shuck the oysters yourself, have the fish merchant at your local store do it. Just ask them to let you keep the bottom halves of the shells! Keep the oyster meats refrigerated until ready to use.

Amy's Note: While cooking, I suggest listening to your favorite "RUH-GAAY" music.

STAUB

Welcome Back Scumbag Scallops Linguine

We love when "Paterson Dolores" shows up and shows out, and this meal delivers just like this gorgeous Jersey Housewife. When Danielle came back on the scene and reconnected with Teresa, she was quick to throw Dolores under the bus, saying Dolores had told her that all Teresa cares about is money. Dolores retorted by calling Danielle a liar and welcoming her back to the group by saying "Welcome back, scumbag!" Cook this with one eye open because this dish is up to no good.

SERVES 4 **PREP TIME:** 10 minutes **COOK TIME:** 20 minutes **TOTAL TIME:** 30 minutes

---

Kosher salt
¾ pound (340 g) linguine
2 tablespoons olive oil
5 tablespoons (75 g) unsalted butter
12 large sea scallops
1 teaspoon sea salt
½ teaspoon freshly ground black pepper
Juice of 2 lemons
3 tablespoons finely chopped fresh parsley
1½ cups (200 g) frozen peas

Chef Stuart's Tip:
Make sure that your scallops are bone-dry so you can achieve a nice golden brown sear on them.

1. Preheat the oven to 200°F (95°C).

2. Bring a large pot of salted water to a boil. Add the linguine and cook according to the package directions, less 1 minute for al dente. Reserve 2 tablespoons of the pasta cooking water and drain the rest. Return to the pot and toss with 1 tablespoon of the oil and cover to keep warm.

3. Meanwhile, in a large nonstick skillet, heat 1 tablespoon of the butter and the remaining 1 tablespoon olive oil over medium-high heat. Pat the scallops dry with a paper towel and season with salt and pepper. Add half of the scallops to the skillet and cook for 2 minutes on each side. Set aside on a sheet pan. Repeat with 2 tablespoons of the butter and the other half of the scallops. Place in the oven to keep warm.

4. Add the lemon juice and 2 tablespoons of the parsley to the skillet with the reserved pasta water. Simmer and reduce for 2 minutes. Add the remaining 2 tablespoons butter and the peas.

5. Add the buttery lemon sauce to the drained pasta and toss.

6. Divide the pasta among four plates and top with the scallops. Garnish with the remaining 1 tablespoon parsley.

Amy's Note: This is ideal to serve to a starving, hungry bitch.

Poto-mac 'n' Cheese with Crab

Maryland is known for its crab, and now it's known for its Housewives, thanks to the elite cast of women who make up *The Real Housewives of Potomac*. One of the newest cities to join the franchise, it has quickly become a classic staple to our *Housewives* diet, much like a good mac and cheese. Since Potomac is all about the class, we're taking this dish to a fancy new level and adding a taste of Maryland crab.

SERVES 6 TO 8 **PREP TIME:** 15 minutes **COOK TIME:** 30 minutes **TOTAL TIME:** 45 minutes

---

Kosher salt
1 pound (450 g) elbow macaroni
1 teaspoon olive oil
1 stick (4 oz/115 g) unsalted butter
1 medium onion, minced
4 cloves garlic, minced
⅓ cup (45 g) all-purpose flour
2½ cups (600 ml) whole milk
1 teaspoon kosher salt
½ teaspoon freshly ground black pepper
½ teaspoon smoked paprika
1½ cups (125 g) shredded sharp white cheddar cheese
½ cup (50 g) shredded mozzarella cheese
½ cup (45 g) grated parmesan cheese
1 pound (450 g) lump crabmeat
1 tablespoon chopped fresh chives
2 cups (215 g) panko bread crumbs, toasted

1. Preheat the oven to 375°F (190°C).

2. Bring a large pot of salted water to a boil. Add the pasta and cook according to the package directions, less 1 minute for al dente. Drain, return to the pot, and toss with the oil to prevent sticking.

3. In a large skillet, melt the butter over medium heat. Add the onion and garlic and cook until softened, 3 to 5 minutes. Whisk in the flour until a paste begins to form. Add the milk and stir in the salt and pepper. Whisking constantly, simmer the sauce until thickened and you no longer see lumps, 2 to 3 minutes. Whisk in the smoked paprika.

4. In a medium bowl, toss together the cheddar, mozzarella, and parmesan. Add half of the cheese to the sauce and stir until melted, about 2 minutes. Add the remaining cheese, reduce the heat to low, and stir until all the cheese has melted and the sauce is smooth. Remove from the heat.

5. Stir the cooked pasta and lump crabmeat into the cheese sauce and pour the mixture into a deep 13 × 9-inch (33 × 23 cm) baking dish.

recipe continued on page 136

Chef Stuart's Tip:
The panko adds a satisfying crunch to this dish—like how this new-ish *Housewives* adds beautiful texture to the franchise.

6. In a small bowl, combine the chives and panko and sprinkle on top of the mac and cheese.

7. Transfer to the oven and bake until the bread crumbs are golden brown, 12 to 15 minutes. Remove the baking dish from the oven and serve the mac and cheese on plates. Enjoy while binge-watching *Potomac* from the beginning.

Amy's Note: Let's be clear, this is not Great Falls Mac 'n' Cheese, it's Poto-mac 'n' Cheese.

Bass Lake Seabass

Bass has never been so dramatic! Tamra was fishing for answers when she questioned Gretchen about taking a trip to Bass Lake while her ill husband was at home by himself. Yikes, talk about awkward. The tension was so thick you couldn't even reel it in. But we're reeling in this fish dish to bring Bass Lake to your plate. The only accusation your friends will make is that you had a bass dinner. Don't flake on this, it's perfect for a summer couples' dinner.

SERVES 4 **PREP TIME:** 10 minutes **COOK TIME:** 10 minutes **TOTAL TIME:** 20 minutes

---

¾ cup (45 g) finely chopped fresh cilantro
Juice of 2 limes
1 teaspoon red wine vinegar
1 teaspoon sugar
1 shallot, finely chopped
1 red Fresno chile or jalapeño pepper, finely chopped
⅓ cup (80 ml) olive oil, plus 1 tablespoon
Kosher salt
4 seabass fillets (6 ounces/170 g each)
Freshly ground black pepper
You Stole My Goddamn House Salad (page 93), for serving

Chef Stuart's Tip: To ensure crispy skin, dry the fillets with a paper towel before seasoning them with salt. Don't put too much oil into the frying pan and make sure it has a chance to get hot before adding the fillets; otherwise, the fish will soak it up and be an oily mess.

1. In a bowl, combine the cilantro, lime juice, vinegar, sugar, shallot, Fresno chile, ⅓ cup of the oil, and ½ teaspoon salt. Set aside.

2. Pat the fish dry with a paper towel and season with salt.

3. In a nonstick skillet, heat the remaining 1 tablespoon of oil over medium heat. Add the fish and cook until opaque in the center, 3 to 4 minutes on each side.

4. Place the fish in the center of a plate and spoon the relish on top. Serve with You Stole My Goddamn House Salad.

Amy's Note: This is the perfect light dish to enjoy before getting "naked wasted."

Fish Room Cioppino

Room assignments among Housewives have always been complicated, but this recipe is straightforward. When visiting Dorinda's Berkshires home, Luann really diva'd out by refusing to stay in the room where sharks and fish adorned the walls. Lu considered it an insult that she was assigned to sleep with the fishes and Dorinda's feelings were hurt. Luann may not be fond of the Fish Room, but we're certain this fish stew will stand up to the Countess's expectations. And, for the record, we would be honored to stay in any room at Blue Stone Manor. We would actually *like* to stay in the fish room, Dorinda. We promise we'll bring dinner!

SERVES 4 UNGRATEFUL GUESTS **PREP TIME:** 10 minutes **COOK TIME:** 20 minutes **TOTAL TIME:** 30 minutes

---

3 tablespoons olive oil
1 medium onion, diced
6 cloves garlic, roughly chopped
1 teaspoon kosher salt
1 teaspoon freshly ground black pepper
2 teaspoons red pepper flakes
1½ cups (360 ml) dry white wine (Chardonnay is best)
1 (28 oz/800 g) can diced San Marzano tomatoes
1½ pounds (700 g) seafood (see Chef Stuart's Tip)
10 fresh basil leaves, chopped, for garnish
1 French baguette, torn into 3-inch (7.5 cm) pieces, for serving
Butter, for serving

Amy's Note: By the way, Bethenny cannot stay in the Fish Room because she's allergic to fish! Also, fair warning, Bethenny—this dish is *not* for you.

1. In a large Dutch oven or heavy pot, heat the oil over medium heat. Stir in the onion and garlic and cook until softened, 3 to 4 minutes. Add the salt, black pepper, and pepper flakes and cook for 1 minute.

2. Add the wine and simmer for 2 minutes. Add the tomatoes and 1 cup (240 ml) water, cover, and let simmer over medium heat for 10 minutes to allow the flavors to meld.

3. Uncover and add the seafood, give a quick stir, re-cover, and cook until the fish just flakes with a fork and any shells have opened, about 5 minutes.

4. Ladle into big bowls, sprinkle with the basil, and serve with the crusty bread and butter.

Chef Stuart's Tip: Instead of sharks and swordfish, try a combination of cod, halibut, mussels, and scallops. Cut the cod and halibut into 2-inch (5 cm) pieces.

Who Said That Sesame Salmon

Time to grill your salmon like Kandi was grilled at the dinner when Marlo asked her if she was a lesbian. That was the rumor anyway, but who said it? No one wanted to admit to it, especially Porsha, who *did* say it. At that fateful dinner, Kandi, Marlo, and Porsha all sounded off in a chorus of "Who said that?" Porsha stuck to her own version of the truth like this salmon sticks to the plank. Fire up your grill and find your own truth in the flames (and, you know, a damn delicious dish, too!).

SERVES 4 **PREP TIME:** 10 minutes **COOK TIME:** 15 minutes **TOTAL TIME:** 1 hour 40 minutes (includes 1 hour soaking and 15 minutes marinating time)

---

4 cedar planks (5 × 11 inches/13 × 28 cm)
3 tablespoons soy sauce
1 tablespoon sesame oil
1 tablespoon white wine vinegar
2 cloves garlic, minced
1 tablespoon minced fresh ginger
1 cup (20 g) chopped fresh cilantro, plus more for garnish
4 skin-on salmon fillets (6 oz/170 g each)
2 cedar grilling planks
1 tablespoon toasted sesame seeds, for garnish
2 scallions, thinly sliced, for garnish
Rice and steamed sugar snap peas, for serving

1. Soak the cedar planks in warm water for 1 hour. Place something heavy on top to keep them submerged in the water.

2. Preheat a gas grill to medium-high heat. If using charcoal, arrange the coals for medium-high direct heat and open the vents. (For oven cooking, see Chef Stuart's Tip.)

3. In a medium bowl, whisk together the soy sauce, sesame oil, vinegar, garlic, ginger, and cilantro.

4. Pour one-quarter of the marinade into a baking dish, place the salmon in the marinade skin side up, and then pour the remaining marinade over the salmon and let it sit for 15 minutes.

5. Place 2 salmon fillets on each cedar plank and grill with the lid on until the salmon is cooked through, 12 to 15 minutes.

6. Sprinkle with the sesame seeds, scallions, and cilantro. Serve with rice and steamed sugar snap peas.

Chef Stuart's Tip: If you're feeling indulgent, you can always soak the planks in wine, sake, or cider to intensify the flavor. For oven cooking, preheat the oven to 375°F (190°C) and bake the salmon for 12 to 15 minutes. Turn on the broiler and cook until nicely charred but not burnt (watch the salmon closely when broiling so it doesn't burn), about 2 minutes.

PAGE 147

POLENTA, PASTA, AND PIZZA

"I run with a fabulous circle of pizza . . . and pasta."

If you don't love pizza, pasta, and *Housewives,* are you even living? Twirl your fork around these great pastas and you'll want to "Mention It Allllll-fredo" (page 159). And like our carb-y creations, the Housewives can be cooked, drained, saucy, and *always* al dente. Still hungry for more? Toss your husband in the pool and have some polenta. *Still* hungry? Okay. Just remember: Brandi's pizza may have been slapped onto the floor, but we're slapping together one heck of a pizza for your next poker party.

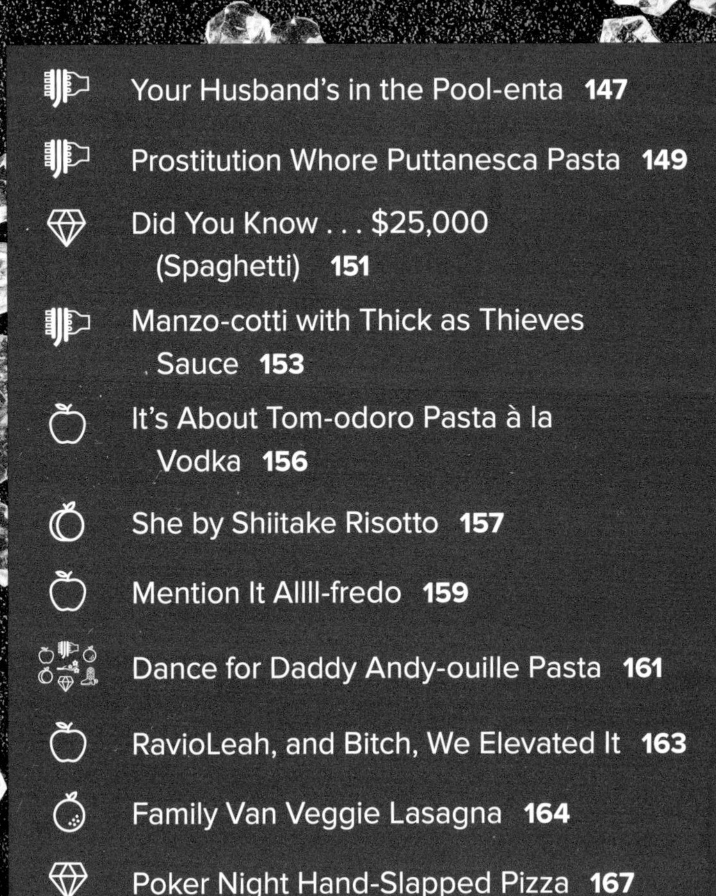

Your Husband's in the Pool-enta

The New Jersey Season 9 finale ended with a splash . . . literally. Danielle's husband, Marty, insulted Marge's looks *again,* but the "powerhouse in pigtails" turned that man into mush by pushing him in the pool. Margaret sauntered away and uttered this iconic line to Danielle, "Yuh husband's in the pool." Danielle was not happy and would eventually seek revenge for this (see Ponytail Pull-ed Pork, page 85). The lesson here is: Don't mess with The Marge, but please do mess with this mush.

SERVES 4 **PREP TIME:** 15 minutes **COOK TIME:** 45 minutes **TOTAL TIME:** 1 hour

4 tablespoons olive oil
1½ pounds (680 g) hot Italian sausage, casings removed
2 carrots, roughly chopped
1 medium onion, chopped
4 cloves garlic, minced
1 bay leaf
½ cup (120 ml) red wine
1 (28 oz/800 g) can whole peeled San Marzano tomatoes
¼ cup (5 g) chopped fresh parsley
¼ cup (60 ml) heavy cream
2 teaspoons kosher salt
2 cups (320 g) polenta
1 cup (90 g) grated parmesan cheese

Amy's Note: You'll have no regrets about diving into this dish!

1. In a large skillet, heat 2 tablespoons of the oil over medium-high heat. Add the sausage and cook until browned, 7 to 10 minutes. Remove from the pan and set aside.

2. Add the carrots, onion, garlic, and bay leaf to the skillet and cook until the vegetables begin to soften, 3 to 6 minutes. Add the wine and let simmer for 2 minutes. Add the tomatoes and crush them with a potato masher, and simmer for 10 minutes. Stir in the parsley, cream, and sausage. Set aside and cover to keep warm.

3. Meanwhile, in a large saucepan, bring 8 cups (1.9 liters) water to a boil, season with the salt and the remaining 2 tablespoons oil. While whisking constantly, add the polenta in four batches so it does not clump. Reduce the heat to a simmer and cook, stirring frequently, until the polenta has thickened, 25 to 30 minutes. Stir in ¾ cup of the parmesan.

4. Spoon the polenta onto a large round plate and make a well in the middle of the polenta. Fill the well with the meat sauce, just like a "POOL," and throw the rest of the parMANesan cheese on top! Enjoy.

Prostitution Whore Puttanesca Pasta

What better way to honor this iconic Teresa/Danielle moment than with a little bit of food history? Pay attention puh-lease! "Puttanesca" comes from the Italian word *puttana,* which means "prostitute." The origin story is that it was created to lure customers with its tantalizing aroma. Listen, when a Housewife calls another Housewife a "prostitution whore," you've got to make a sauce out of it. Enjoy with your friends nineteen times! Or serve at your next book club while reading *Cop Without a Badge* and flipping the table once you're done.

SERVES 4 TO 6 **PREP TIME:** 10 minutes **COOK TIME:** 20 minutes **TOTAL TIME:** 30 minutes

---

Kosher salt
¼ cup (60 ml) olive oil
½ teaspoon red pepper flakes
4 cloves garlic, roughly chopped
1 teaspoon anchovy paste or 2 anchovy fillets, minced
1 tablespoon tomato paste
1 (28 oz/800 g) can whole peeled San Marzano tomatoes, drained
Freshly ground black pepper
¾ cup (135 g) pitted black olives, halved
¼ cup (30 g) capers, drained
1 pound (450 g) pappardelle pasta
Chopped fresh basil, for garnish

Amy's Note: Only two things are true about this recipe: name change. It got arrested (because it's so good).

1. Bring a large pot of salted water to a boil for the pasta.

2. Meanwhile, in a large skillet, combine the oil, pepper flakes, garlic, anchovy paste, and tomato paste and stir over medium heat for 2 to 3 minutes to release their flavors.

3. Add the canned tomatoes to the skillet and crush with a potato masher. Season with ½ teaspoon salt and some pepper. Increase the heat to medium-high and cook the tomatoes to combine the flavors, 3 to 5 minutes. Stir in the olives and capers. Keep the sauce warm until the pasta is ready.

4. Drop the pasta into the boiling water and cook according to the package directions, less 1 minute for al dente.

5. Drain the pasta and add it to the skillet with the sauce, tossing well to combine everything. Toss in the basil and serve.

Chef Stuart's Tip: We made this dish extra classy by using pappardelle instead of the usual spaghetti or linguine. You could also try bucatini.

Did You Know . . . $25,000 (Spaghetti)

The Beverly Hills ladies certainly aren't known for being modest, but Dana Wilkey really took it to the next level at Adrienne's barbecue where we can confidently say that *no* humble pie was served. At the barbecue, the gals mixed and mingled but Dana dominated with all the details regarding her newest bling—her sunglasses that she was proud to say cost a whopping $25,000. So you know what? If Dana can brag about her gold-and-diamond-encrusted sunglasses, then we give ourselves permission to brag about this opulent pasta. Did You Know . . . $25,000 (Spaghetti) might not have diamonds in it, you can trust that it is rich, with decadent ricotta and a heap of parmesan making for a luxurious sauce, and beets providing its beautiful garnet hue. Make sure to serve with a 24-carat-gold fork for maximum bragging rights.

SERVES 4 TO 6 **PREP TIME:** 20 minutes **COOK TIME:** 15 minutes **TOTAL TIME:** 35 minutes

---

Kosher salt
3 medium red beets, peeled
½ cup (120 ml) olive oil
10 ounces (280 g) ricotta cheese
½ cup (45 g) grated parmesan cheese
Juice of 1 lemon
1 pound (450 g) spaghetti or bucatini
2 tablespoons chopped fresh basil leaves, for serving
Shaved parmesan cheese, for serving
½ cup (65 g) pistachios, for serving

Amy's Note: Don your most expensive pair of sunglasses while eating to ensure that everyone around you knows your net worth.

1. Bring a large pot of salted water to a boil for the pasta.
2. Meanwhile, grate the beets on the large holes of a box grater.
3. In a large skillet, heat the oil over medium-high heat. Add the beets and cook until softened, 4 to 5 minutes. Add ¼ cup (60 ml) warm water and cook until the water has evaporated, 2 to 3 minutes. Transfer the beets to a food processor and process to a paste. Add the ricotta, parmesan, and lemon juice and pulse a couple more times until well combined.
4. Meanwhile, cook the pasta according to the package directions, less 1 minute for al dente. Reserve 1 cup (240 ml) of the pasta water, and drain the spaghetti.
5. Toss the spaghetti with the pink ricotta/parmesan mixture and ½ cup (120 ml) of the pasta water. If you want it saucier, add more pasta water.
6. Serve on large white plates and sprinkle with the basil, shaved parmesan, and pistachios.

Chef Stuart's Tip: This is a great recipe for kids, as they'll go wild for the pink color without realizing they're being tricked into eating veggies!

Manzo-cotti

WITH THICK AS THIEVES SAUCE

Lemme tell you somethin' about this dish! Just like Caroline, it is traditional and strong and commands respect. This is the kind of meal that we envision preparing in the Manzos' kitchen, stuffing the shells with Caroline and the gang. If you want to bring your loved ones closer, serve this with the Thick as Thieves Sauce. There's no ham in this recipe so save your cold cuts to play the "Ham Game" with your friends. Teresa can call me "a rat," because I'm telling everyone that this homestyle meal is to die for.

SERVES 6 **PREP TIME:** 25 minutes **COOK TIME:** 35 minutes **TOTAL TIME:** 1 hour

---

3 tablespoons olive oil, plus more for brushing
1 medium onion, diced
½ pound (225 g) ground beef (85% lean)
½ pound (225 g) Italian sausage, casings removed
2 cloves garlic, chopped
½ teaspoon red pepper flakes
1 teaspoon dried oregano
Kosher salt
8 ounces (225 g) manicotti shells
2 cups (500 g) ricotta cheese
¼ teaspoon freshly ground black pepper
3 cups (345 g) shredded mozzarella cheese
1 cup (90 g) grated parmesan cheese, plus more for serving
3 cups (720 ml) Thick as Thieves Sauce (page 155) or your favorite marinara sauce

Amy's Note: Shave your face like Caroline and then shave some fresh parmesan on top.

1. Preheat the oven to 375°F (190°C).
2. In a large skillet, heat 2 tablespoons of the oil over medium heat. Add the onion, beef, and sausage and cook until browned, 8 to 10 minutes. Stir in the garlic, pepper flakes, and oregano. Transfer to a large bowl and let cool.
3. Bring a large pot of salted water to a boil and cook the manicotti for 3 minutes less than the package directions. Drain the manicotti and arrange on a baking sheet brushed with oil and let cool.
4. In a medium bowl, mix together the ricotta, pepper, ½ teaspoon salt, half the mozzarella, and half the parmesan. Stir the cheese mixture into the beef mixture.
5. Brush a 13 × 9-inch (33 × 23 cm) baking dish with the remaining 1 tablespoon oil. Spoon 1 cup (240 ml) of the Thick as Thieves Sauce onto the bottom of the dish.
6. Fill a gallon-size zip-top bag with the beef and cheese mixture, snip a corner, and pipe it into each end of the manicotti shells. Arrange the stuffed shells in the baking dish in one even layer. Spoon the rest of the tomato sauce on top and sprinkle with the leftover cheeses.
7. Bake until the cheese starts to brown on top, 20 to 25 minutes.
8. Let cool for 5 minutes before serving.

Chef Stuart's Tip: Make sure the manicotti cools completely before piping in the filling as the shells can break easily from the heat.

Thick as Thieves Sauce

Caroline stands with her "fambily" and we stand with this sauce. When the Matriarch of New Jersey faced off with Danielle she told her that her family was "as thick as thieves." We're honoring that by making sure this Italian sauce is thick and authentic. Caroline, we know that Teresa insulted you in her cookbook, but don't worry, we insult *everyone* in ours.

MAKES 3 CUPS **PREP TIME:** 5 minutes **COOK TIME:** 20 minutes **TOTAL TIME:** 25 minutes

---

4 tablespoons (60 g) unsalted butter
½ medium onion, diced
1 (28 oz/800 g) can whole peeled San Marzano tomatoes
½ teaspoon red pepper flakes
½ teaspoon kosher salt

Chef Stuart's Tip:
If you find the sauce is too acidic, try adding in a teaspoon or so of sugar to balance it.

1. In a saucepan, melt the butter over medium heat. Add the onion and cook until translucent, 5 to 6 minutes.

2. Add the tomatoes, pepper flakes, and salt, and reduce the heat to medium-low. Crush the tomatoes using a potato masher, and simmer for 15 minutes to thicken and develop the flavors.

Amy's Note: This sauce is like "fambily" to us, and we will protect it at all costs, so make this with respect and integrity.

It's About Tom-odoro Pasta à la Vodka

We all unfortunately remember when Bethenny told Luann that her "soulmate" was making out with another woman at the Regency Hotel. Luann pleaded, "Please don't let it be about Tom." Welp, it was. The tension in this scene was palpable and now it's plateable. Luann tried to make the relationship work despite these findings and went ahead with the wedding. In the end, the pasta didn't stick to the wall, and they got a divorce seven months later. By the way, if you don't love this exquisite dish, I'll be texting you: "How could you do this to me . . . question mark."

SERVES 4 TO 6 **PREP TIME:** 10 minutes **COOK TIME:** 20 minutes **TOTAL TIME:** 30 minutes

---

Kosher salt
¼ cup (60 ml) extra-virgin olive oil
1 shallot, diced
3 cloves garlic, roughly chopped
¼ cup (55 g) tomato paste
2 tablespoons vodka
½ cup (110 g) tomato puree/ passata
½ teaspoon red pepper flakes
¾ cup (180 ml) heavy cream
1 pound (450 g) fusilli pasta, or your favorite pasta
4 tablespoons (60 g) unsalted butter
¾ cup (70 g) finely grated parmesan cheese, plus extra for serving
1 cup (20 g) fresh basil leaves, chopped

1. Bring a large pot of salted water to a boil for the pasta.

2. Heat the oil in a large saucepan over medium heat. Add the shallot and cook for 2 to 3 minutes. Add the garlic and cook for 1 more minute. Stir in the tomato paste and cook for 1 to 2 minutes. Add the vodka and cook until it has evaporated. Add the tomato puree and red pepper flakes and simmer for 8 to 10 minutes. Stir in the cream.

3. Drop the pasta into the pot of boiling water and cook according to the package directions, less 1 minute for al dente.

4. Stir the butter and parmesan into the sauce until all has melted, about 1 minute. Stir in the basil.

5. Drain the pasta and stir into the creamy pink sauce. Serve with extra parmesan.

Chef Stuart's Tip: Yes, I admit, I was drunk when I made this, but I have no regrets because this recipe is one of my go-to, no-fail pasta dishes that you should learn how to make drunk or sober! It's so simple and delicious.

She by Shiitake Risotto

Shiitakes are not quite magic mushrooms, so they can't bring back Shereé's athleisure line. They can, however, make a rich and hearty meal. She by Shereé may be gone, but this risotto is here to stay. It is so warm and cozy, it's like "joggers" for your tummy. This hearty meal will feed your soul like Shereé has fed ours for so long.

SERVES 4 TO 6 **PREP TIME:** 15 minutes **COOK TIME:** 45 minutes **TOTAL TIME:** 1 hour

8 cups (1.9 liters) chicken stock
2 tablespoons olive oil
2 tablespoons (30 g) unsalted butter
2 shallots, finely diced
2 cloves garlic, minced
1 pound (450 g) shiitake mushrooms, sliced
2 cups (400 g) Arborio rice
2 teaspoons fresh thyme leaves, chopped
¾ cup (180 ml) Chardonnay
½ cup (45 g) grated parmesan cheese
1 teaspoon kosher salt
½ teaspoon freshly ground black pepper
Extra-virgin olive oil, for drizzling

Amy's Note: Risotto takes a long time to make, much like the construction of Chateau Shereé, but trust us, it's worth the wait.

1. In a large saucepan, heat the chicken stock over low heat to keep warm.

2. Meanwhile, in a large pot or Dutch oven, heat the 2 tablespoons olive oil and butter over medium heat. Add the shallots and garlic and cook until softened, 2 minutes.

3. Add the mushrooms and cook until browned slightly, 4 to 6 minutes. Scoop the mushrooms out of the pan and set aside (if you end up grabbing some shallots and garlic with the mushrooms, that's okay).

4. Increase the heat to medium-high. Stir in the rice and thyme and keep stirring until the rice is well coated. Add the wine and cook until it looks like all the wine has evaporated.

5. Reduce to medium heat. While maintaining a simmer, ladle about 1 cup (240 ml) of stock into the rice and stir to combine. When the rice has absorbed the stock, add another 1 cup (240 ml) of stock. Keep doing this until the rice is cooked al dente. This should take 18 to 22 minutes. Do not walk away from the pot and keep stirring slowly.

6. Stir in the parmesan and half the cooked mushrooms. If you think the risotto looks a bit dry, you can always add ½ cup (120 ml) or so of stock. Season with the salt and pepper.

7. Serve in bowls topped with the remaining shiitakes. Drizzle with some extra-virgin olive oil.

8. Put on your joggers and enjoy.

Mention It Allll-fredo

Bethenny, the queen of catchphrases, did it again during a Berkshires blowout. Ramona was trying to bring Bethenny's skeletons out of the closet, but her plan backfired. Bethenny wasn't intimidated and in fact invited her to "mention it all!" Ramona vehemently listed Bethenny's indiscretions—topless in a movie, kissed a woman, dated men for their money—and *then* proclaimed that her Skinnygirl brand is done. Emotions were running high and the tension was as creamy and thick as a yummy Alfredo. Don't worry, though, Chef Stuart is going to mention *all* the ingredients you need to make this delicious Alfredo.

SERVES 4 TO 6 **PREP TIME:** 5 minutes **COOK TIME:** 20 minutes **TOTAL TIME:** 25 minutes

---

Kosher salt
1 pound (450 g) fettucine
5 tablespoons (75 g) unsalted butter
1 cup (90 g) finely grated parmesan cheese
1 cup (135 g) frozen peas, thawed
2 cups (280 g) shredded rotisserie chicken
Freshly ground black pepper

Amy's Note: For a dramatic presentation, place two breadsticks in a V shape to re-create Bethenny's iconic leg split.

1. Bring a large pot of salted water to a boil. Add the pasta and cook according to the package directions, less 1 minute for al dente.

2. Reserve ¾ cup (180 ml) of the pasta cooking water from the pasta pot and drain the pasta. Add the pasta water to a large skillet. Bring the water to a simmer over medium-high heat and add the butter. Stir until melted. Stir in the parmesan and keep stirring until all is melted. Add the peas and chicken. If you feel the mixture is too thick, add some more pasta water.

3. Add the pasta to the skillet, and keep tossing until completely coated in the sauce. Sprinkle with a good tablespoon of freshly ground black pepper.

Chef Stuart's Tip: This recipe is awesome, as you can incorporate anything into it. Toss in some peas, chopped asparagus, cooked chicken, shrimp, etc. Whatever you dream up, it can work in this dish. Oh, and one more thing for you Olive Garden fans who think heavy cream is a requirement for an Alfredo sauce: Traditionally, this sauce is made with butter and parmesan cheese, which when melted gives the dish its rich flavor.

ANDY COHEN

Dance for Daddy Andy-ouille Pasta

We give all the props and honors to the highest royalty above all the Housewives, Sir Andy Cohen. The man who makes it all possible for us to indulge in the lives of these compelling women. Not only does he hold his cards and ask the hard-hitting questions, but he has earned his stripes by getting into the mix of the Housewives. He's been pushed by Teresa, kissed by Tamra, and given the name "Silver Bullet" by Kandi. And most important, he was celebrated by *all* the Housewives when they danced for him at his baby shower. Rinna said it best, "Get on a table and dance, you f$*kers!" So do it! Make this dish, then jump up and party for Andy. Invite all your friends to your own "Clubhouse" and seeeeeeerve!

SERVES 4 **PREP TIME:** 10 minutes **COOK TIME:** 25 minutes
TOTAL TIME: 35 minutes

Kosher salt
12 ounces (340 g) penne pasta
2 tablespoons olive oil
10 ounces (285 g) smoked andouille sausage, cut into ¼-inch (6 mm) slices
1 medium onion, diced
2 cloves garlic, minced
1 (20 oz/570 g) can diced San Marzano tomatoes
½ cup (120 ml) heavy cream
2 cups (40 g) arugula
1 cup (90 g) grated parmesan cheese
Freshly ground black pepper

1. Bring a large pot of salted water to a boil. Cook the pasta according to the package directions, less 1 minute for al dente.

2. Meanwhile, in a large skillet, heat the oil over medium-high heat. Add the sausage and cook until browned, 3 to 4 minutes. Remove and set aside.

3. Reduce the heat to medium. Add the onion and garlic to the skillet and cook until softened, about 3 minutes. Add the tomatoes and simmer for 5 to 7 minutes to thicken into a sauce. Stir in the cream, arugula, sausage, and ¾ cup (70 g) of the parmesan until melted. Season with salt and pepper to taste.

4. Drain the pasta, add to the sauce, and stir to coat. Serve with the remaining parmesan and your best dance moves.

Amy's Note: Great for a casual dinner served on couches reunion-style.

Chef Stuart's Tip: Andouille is a smoky sausage that also pairs well in breakfast egg dishes, creamy soups, or rich casseroles.

RavioLeah, and Bitch, We Elevated It

Housewives have always had a knack for throwing food, and Leah proved in her first season to be exemplary at this. At a cozy dinner in a Rhode Island restaurant, an exasperated Leah got tired of overhearing Ramona and Sonja speak poorly of her sister. So she simply took a raviolo from the plate and pitched it, hitting home plate, or rather Ramona, right in the face. Because Leah is a force to be reckoned with, this dish is as well. It's not just ravioli; we took a page from Leah's book and we elevated it with an absolutely mouthwatering sage brown butter sauce.

SERVES 4 TO 6 **PREP TIME:** 5 minutes **COOK TIME:** 20 minutes **TOTAL TIME:** 25 minutes

---

Kosher salt
1 (1 lb/450 g) package frozen cheese ravioli
4 tablespoons unsalted butter
2 cloves garlic, minced
1 dozen fresh sage leaves
Freshly ground black pepper
Grated parmesan cheese, for serving

Chef Stuart's Tip:
Watch the butter carefully when browning, as it can easily burn. I like to use a stainless steel pan because it's easier to see the butter change colors.

1. Bring a large pot of salted water to a boil. Drop in the ravioli and cook according to the package directions.

2. Meanwhile, in a large skillet, melt the butter over medium heat until it begins to turn foamy, 3 to 5 minutes. Add the garlic and sage and keep cooking until the butter begins to turn a golden-brown color. Season with ½ teaspoon salt and ¼ teaspoon pepper and remove from the heat. Add the ravioli and stir to toss in the butter sage sauce.

3. Serve with some parmesan cheese and try not to throw any ravioli at your friends.

Amy's Note: Much like Leah, this dish is a smashing hit that everyone will love. No tiki torches allowed around this meal.

Family Van Veggie Lasagna

A little family van wasn't big enough for The OG of the OC to travel to the airport, so we are making sure that this meal is good enough and big enough for a family of six or more. If you want more of this delicious vegetarian meal, scream at the top of your lungs for more, like Vicki! Get on the fun bus and make this for dinner tonight. Woo-hoo!

SERVES A FAMILY OF 6 **PREP TIME:** 30 minutes **COOK TIME:** 55 minutes
TOTAL TIME: 1 hour 35 minutes (includes 10 minutes resting time)

FOR THE VEGETABLE FILLING

- 2 tablespoons olive oil
- 1 medium onion, diced
- 2 cloves garlic, minced
- ½ teaspoon red pepper flakes
- 3 medium carrots, diced
- 1 red bell pepper, diced
- 1 yellow bell pepper, diced
- 1 zucchini, diced
- 8 ounces (230 g) kale leaves, stemmed

FOR ASSEMBLY

- 2 cups (500 g) ricotta cheese
- ½ cup (45 g) grated parmesan cheese
- ¼ teaspoon kosher salt
- 3 cups (720 ml) tomato sauce, homemade (recipe follows) or store-bought
- 9 no-boil/oven-ready lasagna noodles
- 3 cups (675 g) grated mozzarella cheese

Fresh basil leaves, for garnish

1. Preheat the oven to 400°F (200°C).

2. **MAKE THE VEGETABLE FILLING:** In a large skillet, heat the oil over medium-high heat. Add the onion, garlic, and pepper flakes and cook until softened, 2 to 3 minutes. Reduce the heat to medium. Add the carrots, both bell peppers, and the zucchini and cook until lightly golden, 8 to 10 minutes. Add the kale (in two batches if necessary) and cook until wilted, about 2 minutes. Let cool and pulse in a food processor until it takes on a sauce-like texture.

3. **ASSEMBLE THE LASAGNA:** In a bowl, stir together the ricotta, parmesan, and salt.

4. Spread 1 cup (240 ml) of the tomato sauce on the bottom of a 13 x 9-inch (33 x 23 cm) baking dish. Place 3 noodles side by side over the sauce, overlapping them, if necessary. Spread one-third of the ricotta mixture evenly over the noodles. Layer 1 cup (240 ml) of the vegetable mixture over the ricotta, then sprinkle 1 cup (100 g) of the mozzarella on top. Repeat two more times. You should end up with mozzarella as your final layer.

5. Cover the baking dish with foil. Bake for 20 minutes. Remove the foil and bake until the lasagna is lightly browned, 10 to 15 minutes longer.

6. Remove from the oven and let rest for 10 minutes before serving. Sprinkle with fresh basil.

Chef Stuart's Tip: When preparing the lasagna, don't worry about completely covering the edges of the noodles with your filling and sauce. When the lasagna bakes, everything will come together.

Tomato Sauce

MAKES 3 CUPS (720 ML)

- ¼ cup (60 ml) olive oil
- 2 cloves garlic
- 1 (28 oz/800 g) can whole peeled San Marzano tomatoes
- ½ teaspoon kosher salt
- ¼ teaspoon freshly ground black pepper
- 1 tablespoon chopped fresh basil leaves

In a medium skillet, heat the oil over medium-high heat. Add the garlic and cook for 30 seconds. Add the tomatoes and crush with a potato masher. Add the salt and pepper and simmer, stirring occasionally, for 15 minutes. Stir in the basil. Let cool.

Poker Night Hand-Slapped Pizza

Things seemed pretty innocent when Eileen's husband, Vince, tried to teach the ladies Texas hold 'em, but Kim was loopy and throwing off everyone's game. All bets were off when Kyle pushed Brandi to get to Kim, and in turn Brandi pushed Kyle, so the poor pizza slice landed facedown on Eileen's stone floor. In the end, there was no winning hand in this scenario, especially the pizza. We're picking up the pizza pieces and making a cheesy redemption. No need to roll the dice on this pizza slice—it's a winner.

SERVES 2 OR 3 **PREP TIME:** 15 minutes **COOK TIME:** 30 minutes **TOTAL TIME:** 45 minutes

---

All-purpose flour, for dusting
12 ounces (340 g) store-bought pizza dough, at room temperature
1 tablespoon olive oil
6 slices thick-cut bacon
Kosher salt
½ cup (120 ml) pizza sauce
½ cup (60 g) crumbled Gorgonzola cheese
¾ cup (110 g) shredded rotisserie chicken
4 Medjool dates, pitted and torn
½ teaspoon red pepper flakes
1 cup (20 g) arugula
Extra-virgin olive oil, for drizzling

Amy's Note: This is seriously the best pizza ever. I'm not bluffing.

1. Position a rack in the top third of the oven and preheat the oven to 450°F (230°C).

2. Dust a work surface with flour. Place the dough on the work surface, drizzle with the oil, and stretch to a 10-inch (25 cm) diameter. Cover with plastic wrap.

3. In a 10-inch (25 cm) cast-iron skillet, cook the bacon over medium heat until crisp, 6 to 8 minutes. Set aside and let cool before chopping into 1-inch (2.5 cm) pieces.

4. Pour out the bacon fat and wipe the skillet with a paper towel. Line the skillet with the pizza dough and place the skillet over medium heat. Cook until the dough just starts to brown, 2 to 3 minutes. Remove the pan from the heat.

5. Sprinkle the pizza crust with salt and spread the pizza sauce on top. Sprinkle with the Gorgonzola, bacon, chicken, and dates. Transfer the skillet to the oven and bake until browned in spots, 10 to 13 minutes. Keep a close eye on the pizza and peek in on it like Vince peeked on the feud from the garage window.

6. Let cool and sprinkle with some pepper flakes and top with the arugula. Drizzle with extra-virgin olive oil.

7. Lay the pizza slices atop your poker chips and enjoy.

DUBROW-KEN BOW CHAMPAGNE CUPCAKES
PAGE 171

SWEETS

"If you don't like decadence and class, then go fudge yourself."

Ahhh, dessert. Not exactly the part of the meal that the Housewives often make it to before utensils, dishes, glasses, and insults start hurling across the table. Some goodies even end up in the garbage in Jersey and we call those Trash Sprinkle Cookies (page 185). In fact, it's quite rare to see a Housewife enjoy a sweet treat, with Erika Jayne perhaps a rare exception (see our Pat the Puss-stacio Cream Pie, page 175). But just because the Housewives would rather indulge in a rich argument and a decadent drink toss doesn't mean you shouldn't enjoy these after-dinner attractions!

Dubrow-ken Bow Champagne Cupcakes

Heather's "name change" party took a turn when an uninvited drunk party guest named Sarah broke a piece of the bow off the cake and ate it, claiming she had a sugar problem. Shocked and appalled that her cake with her new initials HD was "defiled," Heather immediately invited Sarah to leave. Sarah was reduced to tears and questioned, "Is this the world we live in? Over a piece of cake?" Well, Sarah, yes, it is, but we've got you covered. Get your sugar fix with these delicious vanilla cupcakes made with Heather's favorite libation, "champs." Just make sure your bows are Dubrow-ken before you serve!

MAKES 24 CUPCAKES **PREP TIME:** 20 minutes **COOK TIME:** 15 minutes
TOTAL TIME: 1 hour (includes 25 minutes assembly time)

FOR THE CUPCAKES

- 1 stick plus 3 tablespoons (150 g) unsalted butter
- 1¾ cups (350 g) granulated sugar
- 3 cups (385 g) all-purpose flour
- 1 tablespoon baking powder
- 1 teaspoon kosher salt
- ¾ cup (180 ml) Champagne
- 5 large egg whites

FOR THE FROSTING

- 12 tablespoons (185 g) unsalted butter, at room temperature
- 1 teaspoon vanilla extract
- 4 cups (480 g) powdered sugar
- 2 tablespoons Champagne
- ½ drop red food coloring

24 sugar bows, for decoration (available online)

Chef Stuart's Tip:
If you can't find or don't want to buy Champagne, feel free to substitute sparkling wine or Prosecco—the bubbles are what's key!

1. **MAKE THE CUPCAKES:** Preheat the oven to 375°F (190°C). Line two standard 12-cup muffin tins with paper liners.
2. In a large bowl, with an electric mixer, cream the butter and granulated sugar together until the mixture looks light and fluffy. In another bowl, combine the flour, baking powder, and salt. Add the flour mixture to the butter and sugar in three additions, alternating with the Champagne, beginning and ending with the flour.
3. In another large clean bowl, whisk the egg whites to stiff peaks. Fold the egg whites into the batter in three batches.
4. Divide the batter among the muffin cups, filling them about three-quarters full.
5. Bake until a toothpick in a cupcake comes out clean, 15 to 17 minutes. Let cool.
6. **MEANWHILE, MAKE THE FROSTING:** In a bowl, with an electric mixer, beat the butter until light. On low speed, beat in the vanilla, 2 cups (240 g) of the powdered sugar, and the Champagne until blended. Beat in the remaining 2 cups (240 g) powdered sugar. Add food coloring to turn the frosting a pinkish color.
7. Frost the cupcakes and place a sugar bow on each.

Life Is a Crème Brûlée

In one of the most dramatic scenes in franchise history, the New York ladies had a fight so explosive, we don't think they made it to the dessert course. We're giving you the dessert they never got. Bethenny and Luann went toe-to-toe in a Miami restaurant over the relentless topic of *Cabaret.* At the apex of this argument, Bethenny had a breakdown, saying that Luann never checked in on her after Dennis died. Bethenny's soliloquy rivaled that of Macbeth's, with her proclaiming, "Life is *not* a cabaret, it is actually not a cabaret!" This scene may have left a bad taste in your mouth, but this crème brûlée is the remedy. And if you don't like this dessert, then you're a "sicko"!

SERVES 4 **PREP TIME:** 15 minutes **COOK TIME:** 40 minutes **TOTAL TIME:** 2 hours 55 minutes (includes chilling and resting time)

1½ cups (360 ml) heavy cream
¾ cup (180 ml) whole milk
2 oranges, zested
1 teaspoon Grand Marnier
8 large egg yolks
½ cup (100 g) sugar
Mint leaves, for garnish
Shortbread cookies, for serving

Amy's Note: I may be slurring my words this dessert is so good. Yes, Luann, I'm having dessert.

1. Preheat oven to 300°F (150°C).

2. In a medium saucepan over medium heat, combine the cream, milk, orange zest, and Grand Marnier and bring to a gentle simmer, then turn off heat. Let cool for 5 to 6 minutes.

3. In a medium bowl, whisk the egg yolks and ¼ cup (50 g) of the sugar together for 1 to 2 minutes, until the yolks are fully incorporated and the mixture is a light yellow.

4. Slowly drizzle ¼ cup at a time of the cream mixture into the egg mixture and whisk; repeat until all the cream is used. Strain mixture through a sieve into a measuring cup.

5. Divide the mixture into four 6-ounce ramekins, place into a baking tray, and fill with warm water 1 inch up the sides of the ramekins.

6. Bake in the center of the oven for 30 to 40 minutes, or until the custard looks set on top.

7. Remove from the oven and let cool completely. Wrap with some plastic wrap and refrigerate for 2 hours or overnight.

8. Remove from the fridge and gently wipe any moisture from the tops with a paper towel. Sprinkle the ramekins with the remaining 4 tablespoons sugar and torch like Bethenny torched Luann until she broke, until brown and crispy. Top each ramekin with a mint leaf and serve with some shortbread cookies.

Pat the Puss-stacio Cream Pie

This "pat-the-puss" pop queen will love our version of pie just for her. It's so rich and creamy, it tastes "XXpen$ive," but it only takes a few dollars to make this showstopping dessert. Erika has given us over-the-top glam looks and musical performances to stop the presses, but she also gave us a slice of realness when she ate store-bought pumpkin pie right out of the tin for breakfast while camping. Who doesn't want pie for breakfast? We sure do!

SERVES 6 TO 8 **PREP TIME:** 20 minutes **TOTAL TIME:** 2 hours 20 minutes (includes 2 hours chilling time)

---

1 (3.4 oz/96 g) box pistachio instant pudding mix, such as Jell-O
¾ cup (180 ml) whole milk
1 cup (240 g) sour cream
2½ cups (600ml) heavy cream
½ cup (60 g) pistachios, roughly chopped
1 store-bought graham cracker crust, or any prebaked store-bought pie crust
¼ cup (25 g) powdered sugar

1. In a bowl, whisk the pudding mix and milk until thickened, about 2 minutes. Stir in the sour cream and 1 cup (240 ml) of the heavy cream with ¼ cup (30 g) of the pistachio. Spoon the mixture into the crust.

2. In a bowl, with an electric mixer, whip the remaining 1½ cups (360 ml) heavy cream with the powdered sugar until it forms stiff peaks. Spoon the cream on top of the pie and sprinkle with the remaining ¼ cup (30 g) pistachios.

3. Refrigerate for 2 hours before serving.

Amy's Note: This pie is Pantygate-dropping good.

Diaper Dump Cake

Lisa Rinna may have done the commercials, but it's our beloved Sonja Tremont Morgan who walks the walk—and talks the shit—when it comes to diapers. We love Sonja for her multitude of eccentricities and honest-to-goodness realness. Donning a diaper for a long bus ride is indeed a unique traveler's tip, and one that we took to heart for this specialty cake. A dump cake typically means "throw whatever you have in it and let it bake." Well, we'll show you how to make it Sonja-style. Sonja said it best when she welcomed Leah to their group: "If you wanna hang with us, you wear diapers."

SERVES 6 TO 8 **PREP TIME:** 20 minutes **COOK TIME:** 50 minutes **TOTAL TIME:** 1 hour 10 minutes

---

3 cups (300 g) sweetened shredded coconut
2 cups (230 g) toasted walnuts, chopped
1 (15.25 oz/432 g) box chocolate cake mix
8 ounces (225 g) cream cheese, at room temperature
1 stick (4 oz/115 g) unsalted butter, at room temperature
1 tablespoon vanilla extract
2 cups (240 g) powdered sugar
2 tablespoons whole milk
½ cup (80 g) semisweet chocolate chips
½ cup (80 g) white chocolate chips

1. Position a rack in the center of the oven and preheat the oven to 375°F (190°C). Butter a 13 x 9-inch (33 x 23 cm) baking pan and line with parchment paper.

2. Sprinkle the coconut and walnuts on the bottom of the pan.

3. Prepare the cake batter according to the package directions. Pour into the pan and spread evenly.

4. In a bowl, with an electric mixer on low speed, beat together the cream cheese, butter, vanilla, powdered sugar, and milk. Stir in both chocolate chips. Using a large ice cream scoop, scoop out rounds the size of golf balls and place on top of the chocolate cake mix. The scoops will sink slightly during baking.

5. Transfer the cake to the oven and bake until slightly firm to the touch, 40 to 50 minutes. Remove and let cool completely.

6. Always keep a Diaper Dump Cake in your bag; you never know when you'll need it.

Amy's Note: Perfect for a retirement party or baby shower. Serve in a diaper. Really.

Diamonds and Rosé Parfait

Life may not be all diamonds and rosé, but nobody ever said anything about a parfait! Lisa Vanderpump, the queen of Beverly Hills, named her pet mini ponies Diamonds and Rosé. So it's only fitting that we name our pet parfait the same. Inspired by a British dessert called Eton Mess, it's perfect because Lisa's nickname is "Pinky" and the strawberries mixed with cream are sure to turn a lovely pinkish hue, a fitting tribute for the brash Brit. A dessert fancy enough to be in any one of Lisa's restaurants or served in her personal olive grove at Villa Rosa, this is also ideal for a tea party dessert with the ladies. Drape yourself in diamonds, pop open the rosé, and serve it like you deserve it.

SERVES 4 TO 6 **PREP TIME:** 15 minutes **TOTAL TIME:** 1 hour 15 minutes (includes 1 hour chilling time)

---

2 cups (400 g) strawberries, hulled and sliced
3 tablespoons sugar
½ cup (120 ml) dry rosé wine
2 tablespoons Monin lavender syrup
3 cups (720 ml) heavy cream
8 ounces (220 g) vanilla meringue cookies

Amy's Note: This parfait is heavy, dahling, so just leave it where it belongs . . . in the center of the table.

1. In a medium bowl, combine the strawberries, sugar, rosé, and lavender syrup and refrigerate for 1 hour.

2. In another medium bowl, with an electric mixer, whip the cream to stiff peaks. Set aside.

3. In a large bowl, lightly crush the meringue cookies. Fold in three-quarters of the whipped cream and stir gently.

4. Set a sieve over a bowl to catch the juices and drain the strawberries. Layer the meringue mixture in the bottom of a large wineglass or an old-fashioned glass. Top with some of the strawberries and a drizzle of the reserved berry juice, then top with the rest of the meringue cream and the rest of the strawberries. Finish with the whipped cream.

Chef Stuart's Tip: You can buy the lavender syrup online. Lavender and strawberries are a match made in heaven.

Candiace's Tears-amisu

A true pageant queen knows how to cry at the drop of a hat, and Candiace is proof of that. We've seen more tears from her in one season than from any other Housewife *ever*. Her crying technique is elegant and beautiful, much like this delicious dessert. It's so good, actually, that you might cry. So prepare your plate and keep a folded and pointed tissue next to you, to do the "Candiace tissue-dab," just in case.

SERVES 4 **PREP TIME:** 30 minutes **TOTAL TIME:** 6 hours 45 minutes (includes 6 hours chilling time)

- **½ cup (50g) unsweetened cocoa powder, plus more for dusting**
- **5 fresh large egg yolks**
- **¾ cup (150 g) sugar**
- **1 cup (240 ml) heavy cream**
- **1 cup (240 g) mascarpone cheese**
- **2 cups (480 ml) very strong coffee, cooled**
- **3 tablespoons Grand Marnier**
- **½ cup (50 g) unsweetened cocoa powder**
- **2 dozen ladyfingers**

Amy's Note: Candiace's tears are salty, but this tiramisu is sweet!

1. Dust an 8-inch (20 cm) square baking dish with cocoa powder. Set aside.

2. In a medium bowl, with an electric mixer, beat together the yolks and ¼ cup (50 g) of the sugar until the egg yolks become pale, about 1 minute.

3. In another bowl, with an electric mixer, beat the cream with the remaining ½ cup (100 g) sugar until you get soft peaks. Add the mascarpone and continue to whip until you achieve medium peaks that are still slightly soft (you want to be able to spread this mixture).

4. Add the egg mixture to the mascarpone and mix together.

5. In a bowl, mix the coffee and Grand Marnier together.

6. Dip both sides of a ladyfinger into the coffee mixture quickly, and place in the bottom of the prepared baking dish. Repeat until the bottom of the dish is covered. You can break the ladyfingers in half if you need to fill some gaps.

7. Spread half the mascarpone mixture on the ladyfingers, filling spaces until you have a smooth top. Dust with cocoa powder. Repeat with the second and final layer of ladyfingers, followed by the remaining mascarpone mixture and a final dusting of cocoa powder. Refrigerate for at least 6 hours or up to overnight.

8. Serve alongside folded napkins in the shape of Candiace's tissues for your guests' tears.

Poop Hat Peach Cobbler

At the Mad Hatter's tea and luncheon charity event, where guests showed off their beautiful, expensive, custom-designed hats to raise money, Brandi showed off her "poop in the park" hat and pissed off LeeAnne. Brandi didn't care about the who's who when she put the poo-poo in her DYI hat. Put it this way: Drama came in the form of a poop hat, and now it's in the form of a cobbler. In the spirit of fun, fart-loving Brandi, this is made in a Dutch oven, get it? Dutch oven? But the flavor of this dessert is not a joke at all. It's crumbly, fruity, and warm and will have you mad as a hatter that you didn't make this sooner. This dessert is perfect for a tea party or for your next Dallas reunion party.

SERVES 6 TO 8 **PREP TIME:** 5 minutes **COOK TIME:** 1 hour 5 minutes **TOTAL TIME:** 1 hour 10 minutes

2 pounds (900 g) frozen sliced peaches
2 cups (400 g) sugar
2 tablespoons fresh lemon juice
½ teaspoon ground cinnamon
1 cup (120 g) all-purpose flour
1 tablespoon baking powder
½ teaspoon kosher salt
1 stick (4 oz/115 g) unsalted butter, melted
1 cup (240 ml) whole milk
Vanilla ice cream, for serving

Chef Stuart's Tip:
This can also be made in a 13 × 9-inch (33 × 23 cm) baking dish if you do not have a Dutch oven. You'd still cook the peaches on the stovetop as instructed, and the baking time would not change.

1. Preheat the oven to 375°F (190°C).

2. In a 5-quart (4.7-liter) Dutch oven, combine the peaches, 1 cup of the (200 g) sugar, the lemon juice, cinnamon, and ¼ cup (60 ml) water and bring to a boil over medium-high heat. Cook, stirring constantly, for 10 minutes to break down the peaches. Set aside and let cool for 10 minutes.

3. In a bowl, whisk together the flour, remaining 1 cup (200 g) sugar, the baking powder, and salt. Stir in the melted butter and milk to make a batter.

4. Pour the batter over the peaches, slide the cobbler into the oven, and bake until set, 30 to 40 minutes. Serve warm with some vanilla ice cream.

Amy's Note: I love exquisite cuisine, but I'm not above a poop joke, and this dessert is a little of both.

Trash Sprinkle Cookies

We love a good cookie feud, and this one between Teresa and Melissa hits our sweet spot. You shouldn't dare bring store-bought sprinkle cookies to your sister-in-law's house on Christmas or else they'll end up in her garbage can. Teresa may have proven a point by tossing Melissa's cookies into the can, but we're certain *these* homemade tasty treats would not suffer the same demise.

MAKES 24 COOKIES **PREP TIME:** 20 minutes **COOK TIME:** 10 minutes **TOTAL TIME:** 30 minutes

---

1¾ cups (220 g) all-purpose flour
1¾ teaspoons baking powder
½ teaspoon kosher salt
1 stick (4 oz/115 g) unsalted butter, at room temperature
1 cup (200 g) sugar
1 large egg
1 teaspoon vanilla extract
½ teaspoon almond extract
¾ cup (220 g) sprinkles

Amy's Note: Bring these sweet treats to your next family event and see if they bring your family together or tear it apart.

1. Preheat the oven to 350°F (175°C). Line two 13 x 9-inch (33 × 23 cm) baking sheets with parchment paper.

2. In a large bowl, whisk together the flour, baking powder, and salt.

3. In a bowl, with an electric mixer, cream the butter and sugar together at high speed until light and pale in color. Turn the speed to medium and add the egg, vanilla, and almond extract. Add the flour mixture in two batches until everything is combined.

4. Pour the sprinkles on a plate and set aside.

5. Using a 1½-tablespoon ice cream scoop, scoop out the dough and lightly roll in the sprinkles. Set the cookies on the baking sheet as you work.

6. Bake until the centers of the cookies still look slightly undercooked (they'll finish cooking from residual heat when taken out of the oven), 8 to 10 minutes.

7. Transfer the cookies onto a wire rack to cool for 15 minutes.

yolanda

Yolanda Bananas Foster

Gather around the Grammy-adorned piano and take in the Malibu view because it's time for dessert! Before *and* after Yolanda was a Hadid, we celebrate when she was a Foster. We invite you to delight in this decadent dessert named after her marriage to musician/songwriter David Foster. The Dutch model and self-proclaimed "hostess with the mostest" prided herself on her elegant "dinter partees" that included a specially designed menu and elaborate tablescapes, complete with place cards (if you were a part of the "Dream Team," you got a heart on your card). With the eclectic mix of musicians and Housewives at these parties, things would surely get bananas . . . and so we're getting bananas now.

SERVES 4 **PREP TIME:** 10 minutes **COOK TIME:** 10 minutes **TOTAL TIME:** 20 minutes

---

4 tablespoons (60 g) unsalted butter
¾ cup (150 g) packed light brown sugar
4 bananas, halved lengthwise
¼ teaspoon ground cinnamon
½ cup (120 ml) brandy
Vanilla ice cream
½ cup (55 g) pecans, roughly chopped

1. In a small skillet, melt the butter and brown sugar over medium-high heat until it starts to darken in color, 5 to 6 minutes. Add the banana halves and sauté until lightly browned on each side, 2 to 3 minutes. Sprinkle with the cinnamon. Remove the pan from the heat.

2. Add the brandy to the bananas in the pan. To flambé, carefully light the sauce with a long-reach lighter. When the flames die out, spoon the bananas onto a plate and top with vanilla ice cream and pecans.

Amy's Note: This dessert is good enough to be in Yolanda's fridge.

Ragamuffins: A Happy Ending Dessert

We turned a hot-mic moment into a hot-buns moment. After Kyle indignantly exited Denise's outdoor buffet dinner, she was caught on a hot mic saying that Denise always looks like a "ragamuffin." Even when Denise was saying "Bravo Bravo f'ing Bravo," we always thought she was as sweet as this dessert. These are so insanely yummy, you'll eat them up faster than Denise left every scene. And as we all know, Denise loves a "happy ending," so save this treat for last. While you are enjoying, please refrain from talking about "threesomes," as there may be kids around.

MAKES 12 RAGAMUFFINS **PREP TIME:** 25 minutes **COOK TIME:** 15 minutes **TOTAL TIME:** 40 minutes

---

2½ cups (325 g) all-purpose flour, plus more for dusting
½ cup (50 g) packed plus 1 tablespoon dark brown sugar
2 teaspoons baking powder
¾ teaspoon kosher salt
6 tablespoons (90 g) cold unsalted butter, cut into cubes, plus 2 tablespoons (30 g), melted
¾ cup (180 ml) whole milk
¼ cup (50 g) granulated sugar
1 tablespoon ground cinnamon
2 cups (250 g) powdered sugar

Chef Stuart's Tip: These cinnamon bun muffin mash-ups are best served with coffee or tea at breakfast.

1. Preheat the oven to 400°F (200°C). Line a 13 x 9-inch (33 × 23 cm) baking sheet with parchment paper.

2. In a large bowl, mix together the flour, 1 tablespoon of the brown sugar, the baking powder, salt, and the 6 tablespoons (90 g) of cubed cold butter. Using your hands, squeeze the butter through the flour mixture until it resembles a crumbly mix. Add the milk and keep kneading until it resembles a dough, 2 to 3 minutes.

3. Dust a surface with some flour and roll out the dough to a roughly 13 × 11-inch (33 × 28 cm) rectangle.

4. Brush the 2 tablespoons (30 g) of melted butter onto the dough. In a bowl, mix together the granulated sugar, remaining ½ cup (50 g) brown sugar, and the cinnamon. Sprinkle three-quarters of the cinnamon sugar mixture onto the dough. Roll up the dough tightly and cut the log crosswise into slices 1½ inches (3.5 cm) wide. Arrange the slices on the lined baking sheet. Sprinkle the remaining cinnamon sugar on top.

5. Bake until golden brown, about 15 minutes. Let cool for 15 minutes.

6. In a bowl, whisk together the powdered sugar and 2 tablespoons water to make an icing. Drizzle generously over the ragamuffins.

Amy's Note: These are so sticky, gooey, and delicious, you'll be happy to end your night with them.

Jill's Tennis Balls

Tennis, anyone? Grab your racket and some delicious dates and let's play some mixed doubles! Our favorite ginger-haired Housewife sure made her mark on RHONY. She showed us that anything is possible in a tennis skirt. When your tennis pro cancels on you, play a psychological game with Ramona and get Simon to be your doubles partner. Whether the games you're playing are physical, mental, or emotional, these healthy treats will be the perfect snack afterwards.

MAKES 12 TO 16 BALLS **PREP TIME:** 15 minutes **TOTAL TIME:** 1 hour 15 minutes (includes 1 hour chilling time)

½ cup (50 g) pistachios
10 Medjool dates, pitted
½ cup (80 g) bittersweet chocolate chips (60% cacao)
Icing (optional)

Chef Stuart's Tip: I love to make a bunch of these and pop one or two for breakfast or before a workout on the tennis court.

1. In a food processor, pulse the pistachios until finely ground. Transfer to a plate.

2. In the food processor, pulse the dates and chocolate chips together until they form a paste that can be rolled.

3. Roll the mixture into 2-tablespoon balls. Roll the balls in the pistachios. If you want, you can also pipe icing onto the balls to resemble tennis balls.

4. Refrigerate for 1 hour to set. Put on your tennis skirt and enjoy.

Amy's Note: The score on these treats is love-love.

Ding Dong Dungeon Cake

The bachelorette party for Cynthia was replete with alter egos and vibrating panties, so who doesn't want a Dungeon party thrown by the Mistress herself, Kandi? We do! This delicious Ding Dong cake is inspired by Bolo the stripper who left the Atlanta ladies speechless at the sight of his ding dong. This cream-filled cake is to be enjoyed at your Dungeon-themed party or in an intimate threesome. When not eating, put in a glass box like Bolo and enjoy later. Mistress says you will eat this cake and love it.

SERVES 8 TO 10 **PREP TIME:** 20 minutes **COOK TIME:** 50 minutes **TOTAL TIME:** 1 hour 45 minutes (includes 15 minutes cooling time and 20 minutes setting time)

FOR THE CAKE

- Cooking spray
- 2 cups (260 g) all-purpose flour
- 2 cups (400 g) sugar
- 1 cup (100 g) unsweetened cocoa powder
- 2 teaspoons instant espresso powder
- 2 teaspoons baking soda
- 1 teaspoon baking powder
- 1½ cups (360 ml) buttermilk
- 6 tablespoons (90 g) unsalted butter, melted
- 2 teaspoons vanilla extract

FOR THE CREAM FILLING

- 1 cup (240 ml) whole milk
- ¾ cup (100 g) all-purpose flour
- ½ teaspoon vanilla extract
- 2 sticks (8 oz/230 g) unsalted butter, at room temperature
- 1 cup (200 g) sugar

1. **MAKE THE CAKE:** Preheat the oven to 350°F (175°C). Mist two 9-inch (23 cm) cake pans with cooking spray.

2. In a bowl, whisk together the flour, sugar, cocoa, espresso powder, baking soda, and baking powder.

3. In another bowl, whisk together the buttermilk, melted butter, and vanilla. Add the wet ingredients to the dry ingredients and mix until well combined.

4. Divide the batter between the prepared pans. Bake until a toothpick inserted in the cake comes out clean, 30 minutes. Let the cakes cool completely on a wire rack.

5. **MAKE THE CREAM FILLING:** In a saucepan, bring the milk to a boil. Reduce the heat to low, whisk in the flour, and keep cooking and mixing until it thickens, kind of like a pudding or custard. Remove from the heat and stir in the vanilla. Let the mixture cool for 15 minutes.

6. In a large bowl, with an electric mixer, cream the butter and sugar together until light and fluffy. Add the cooled milk pudding mixture and keep mixing until it looks like whipped cream. Set aside.

recipe continued on page 194

FOR THE GANACHE TOPPING

¾ cups (180 ml) heavy cream
7 ounces (200 g) semisweet chocolate (60% cacao)

Amy's Note: You don't have to cover the cameras to eat this dessert!

7. **MAKE THE GANACHE TOPPING:** In a saucepan, heat the cream over medium heat until it starts to boil. Remove from the heat and add the chocolate, let sit for 5 minutes, then stir until smooth and set aside.

8. Place a layer of the cooled cake on a large plate or cake stand. Top with the cream filling. Add the second layer of cake. Pour the ganache over the cake and use a spatula to cover the top and sides. Let sit for 15 to 20 minutes for the ganache to set. Serve.

Chef Stuart's Tip: I mentioned making sure your cake was completely cool before frosting—if you don't exercise patience and move forward early, your filling and ganache will melt!

My Motha's Pizzelle

We are talking cookbook drama in a cookbook! How meta! That's what makes this recipe so special to us. Not only is this cookbook drama, it's also family drama, *and* it's food drama. You might remember that Kathy went to support Teresa at her cookbook signing, and she paged through the book impressed but kept saying that recipes were from her mother. "Oh, my motha's pizzelle!" Teresa took offense and said they were her family's recipes. Well, this is Chef Stuart's pizzelle recipe, but we can't lie, it's totally inspired by Kathy's mother's pizzelle.

MAKES 30 TO 40 PIZZELLE **PREP TIME:** 10 minutes **COOK TIME:** 20 minutes **TOTAL TIME:** 30 minutes

---

4 large eggs
1 cup (200 g) granulated sugar
1 teaspoon kosher salt
1 teaspoon vanilla or almond extract
2 cups (260 g) all-purpose flour
2 teaspoons baking powder
1½ sticks (6 oz/170 g) unsalted butter, melted
Vegetable oil
Powdered sugar, for dusting

Amy's Note: The design on this cookie is as complex as the family drama in Jersey. But oh-so-sweet!

1. In a large bowl, whisk together the eggs, granulated sugar, salt, and extract until well mixed.

2. In another bowl, whisk together the flour and baking powder. Add the flour mixture to the egg mixture. Add the melted butter and mix to combine.

3. Grease a pizzelle iron with some vegetable oil on a paper towel, rubbing all over the iron to prevent sticking.

4. Heat the pizzelle iron and cook the pizzelle according to the manufacturer's instructions. (Generally, this takes 1½ to 2 minutes per pizzelle.)

5. Set the pizzelle aside to cool. Dust with powdered sugar.

Chef Stuart's Tip: No Italian American holiday is complete without crisp, buttery pizzelle. This is the perfect holiday treat, because the recipe yields such a big batch (lending itself well to holiday binging)!

Mr. Chocolate Torte

One of the most mysterious romances that kept us asking questions is now a torte that will keep you asking for more. Phaedra's alleged romance with a man she endearingly named "Mr. Chocolate" is as decadent as this dessert. She kept his identity under wraps, but we were titillated to find out years later that this man was rumored to be the ex-husband of Gizelle from Potomac. Some may call it a bittersweet mix-up. You can't write this stuff . . . but now you can cook it!

SERVES 6 TO 8 **PREP TIME:** 25 minutes **COOK TIME:** 35 minutes **TOTAL TIME:** 1 hour

---

FOR THE CAKE

10 chocolate graham crackers, such as Honey Maid
⅓ cup (70 g) sugar
4 tablespoons (60 g) unsalted butter, melted

FOR THE FILLING

1¼ cups (300 ml) heavy cream
10 ounces (200 g) bittersweet chocolate chips (60% cacao is best)
1 teaspoon vanilla extract
2 large eggs
½ cup (65 g) hazelnuts, toasted and chopped
½ teaspoon Maldon sea salt

1. Preheat the oven to 350°F (175°C).

2. **MAKE THE CAKE:** In a food processor, pulse the graham crackers 6 to 8 times. Add the sugar and melted butter and pulse a couple more times, until everything is combined.

3. Pour the mixture into a 10-inch (25 cm) tart pan with a removable bottom and press around the edges of the pan using your fingers.

4. Bake for 12 minutes, remove, and let cool completely. (Leave the oven on.)

5. **MEANWHILE, MAKE THE FILLING:** In a medium saucepan, bring the cream to a boil over medium heat. Remove from the heat and stir in the chocolate chips and vanilla. Let sit for 5 minutes.

6. Whisk in the eggs one at a time. Stir in the hazelnuts and sea salt.

7. When the crust has cooled completely, pour in the filling. Return to the oven and bake until firm, about 15 to 17 minutes.

FOR SERVING

Caramel ice cream
Sea salt

8. Remove the tart from the oven and let cool completely in the pan.

9. Serve with caramel ice cream and a sprinkling of sea salt.

Chef Stuart's Tip: The tart pan with a removable bottom is key here, otherwise you risk the torte messily sticking if using a traditional pan (trust me, I speak from experience!). Make your life sweeter by investing in the tart pan—you won't regret it.

Amy's Note: The legend of this infamous man is layered . . . and so is this dessert.

DRINKS AND COCKTAILS

"I may be the messiest one at the party, but I always tell the truth."

Yes, Luann, we're drinking. Let's be honest: Alcohol is the cast member we can always count on to show up and shake up the drama. More often than not, these liquid contents end up on the table, the floor, or in some cases someone's face (see Cease and Despritzer, page 215). And sometimes even a Housewife is the straw that stirs the drink, like Sonja. In any case, we've got you covered with our extraordinary list of drinks for every occasion and inebriation. Invite your friends over and get ready to Make It Nice Spiced Cider (page 235).

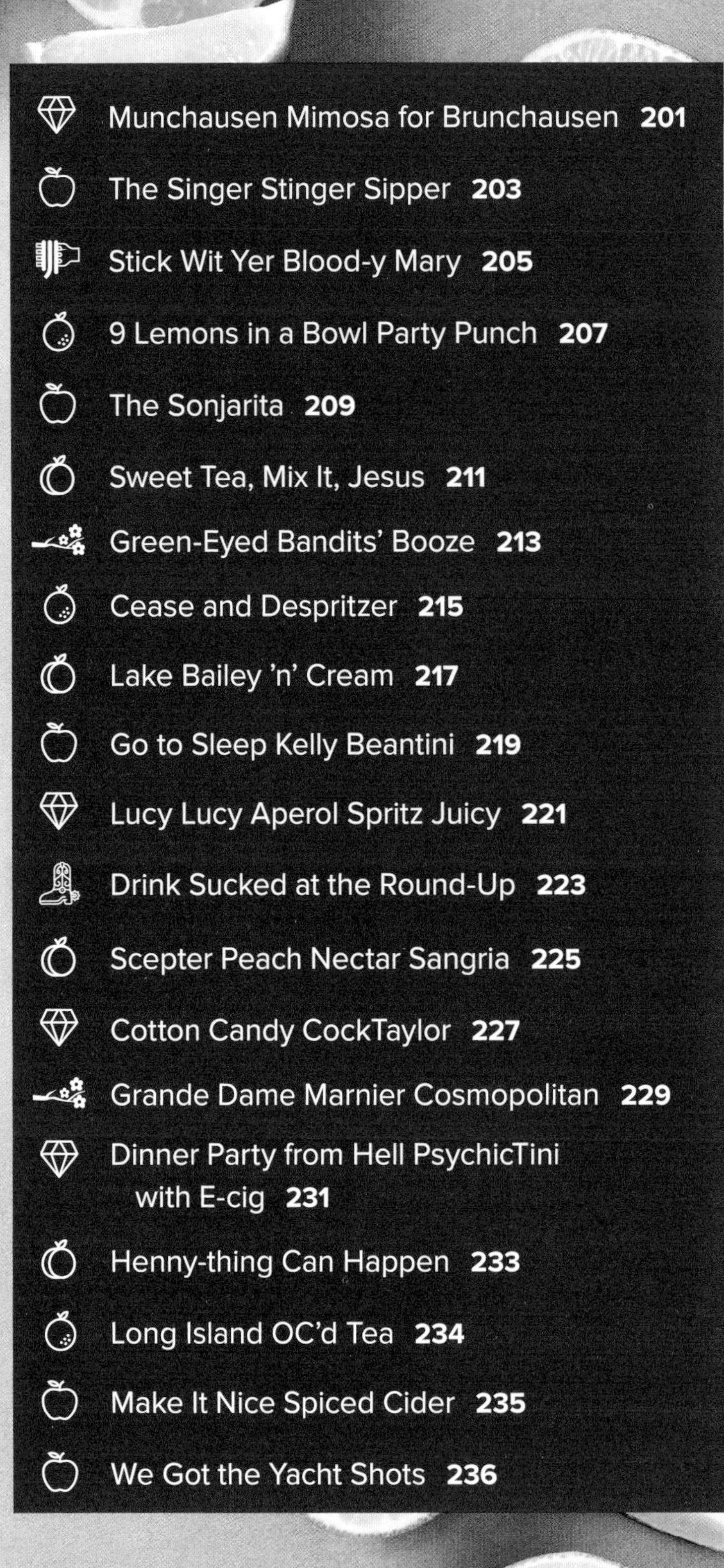

Munchausen Mimosa for Brunchausen

Do you love brunch? Or do you make yourself think you love brunch? I know we have a lot of nerve for asking, but we're drawing inspiration from Rinna's Munchausen query. Rinna boldly went where no Housewife had gone before by questioning the validity of Yolanda's illness, and it ultimately bubbled over like a popped bottle of Dom. Be as bold as Rinna to ask the questions that no one wants to ask and to discuss the forbidden and the improper. No better place to do all that than in the light of day at brunch with this fresh and fabulous mimosa. Our mimosa is the best, so you better believe we're gonna talk about it!

SERVES 1

½ ounce (15 ml) fresh lemon juice
1 teaspoon chopped candied lemon peel
6 ounces (180 ml) Champagne
½ slice candied lemon, for garnish

1. Pour the lemon juice and lemon peel into an 8-ounce (250 ml) Champagne flute.

2. Top up with the Champagne and garnish with the candied lemon slice.

Amy's Note: We added lemon to this so it would cut through the bullshit and honor Yolanda.

The Singer Stinger Sipper

Okay, ya know what? An iconic Housewife calls for an extraordinary drink. Ramona Singer shoots from the hip and has no filter, and some of her remarks sting like a bee. That's why "Holla" Heather gave her the nickname "The Singer Stinger." Of course we made this drink with Pinot Grigio, as it is synonymous with Ramona (she even had her very own brand). We've watched Ramona order a drink on the show countless times, so in the spirit of getting this right, make sure you put it in a tall wineglass with lots of ice and sip with a straw. We sting this drink with some lemons and limes, and we add a splash of sugar for Ramona's sweet "in all sincerity" apologies. Cheers, it's "Turtle Time" somewhere!

SERVES 4 TO 6 **PREP TIME:** 5 minutes **TOTAL TIME:** 35 minutes (includes 30 minutes chilling time)

¼ cup (80 ml) simple syrup (page 207)
1 lemon, thinly sliced
1 lime, thinly sliced
1 bottle (750 ml) Pinot Grigio
10 fresh mint leaves, plus more for garnish
Lime sparkling water

1. In a large pitcher, combine the simple syrup, lemon slices, and lime slices and lightly mix to combine without breaking up the fruit. Add the wine and mint leaves. Let sit in the fridge for 30 minutes.

2. To serve, fill a large wineglass three-quarters full with ice. Pour in the stinger and top with lime sparkling water. Garnish with lots of mint leaves.

Amy's Note: Beware—after a couple of these drinks you might sting someone and the morning after you'll be "The Apologizer."

Stick Wit Yer Blood-y Mary

A family retreat never went quite as badly as the one with the Giudices and the Gorgas. Teresa told her brother to stick with his blood, but Joe said he's not going to stick with scum like her, which brought the two Joes to fisticuffs. When it comes to a good Bloody Mary, you shouldn't be afraid to pile on the garnishes like these families pile on the drama—after all, blood is thicker than tomato juice, but not nearly as tasty with vodka.

SERVES 4 TO 6 **PREP TIME:** 5 minutes **TOTAL TIME:** 10 minutes

---

3 cups (720 ml) tomato juice
1 cup (225 g) canned tomato sauce
1 tablespoon prepared horseradish
2 tablespoons Worcestershire sauce
1 teaspoon celery salt
1 clove garlic, minced
¾ teaspoon freshly ground black pepper
1 cup (240 ml) vodka
Smoked Maldon sea salt, for rimming the glass
1 lime, cut into wedges
Garnishes: Mini meatballs (see Chef Stuart's Tip from Gorga-zola Balls, page 117), pepperoncini, olives, cherry tomatoes, celery stalks, lemon slices, cucumber spears

Amy's Note: This drink will not fix your deep-seated issues with family, but it will certainly cure your hangover.

1. In a large glass pitcher, combine the tomato juice, tomato sauce, horseradish, Worcestershire sauce, celery salt, garlic, pepper, and vodka. Add more vodka if you like!

2. Spread the smoked salt on a plate. Wet the rim of a tall glass with a lime wedge and rim with the salt. Squeeze the lime juice into the glass and drop the wedge into the glass. Fill with ice and top with the Bloody Mary mix.

3. Go crazy with garnishing your Bloody Mary!

Chef Stuart's Tip: Spice it up with a dash of hot sauce! Or take a swig right out of the bottle, just like Nonno.

9 Lemons in a Bowl Party Punch

If we've learned anything from the feng shui–loving, holistic goddess from the OC, it's that "If life gives you lemons, put nine in a bowl." You don't need hospital-grade air in your home or jewels in your teeth to make this—all you need are lemons and a few simple ingredients. If you "start charities" like Shannon, this is a great beverage to serve at a fundraiser.

SERVES 6 TO 8 **PREP TIME:** 15 minutes **TOTAL TIME:** 1 hour 15 minutes (includes 1 hour chilling time)

---

9 lemons
1 cup (240 ml) simple syrup (recipe follows)
2 cups (480 ml) lemon vodka
1 (750 ml) bottle Champagne
Mint sprigs, for garnish

1. Squeeze the juice from 8 of the lemons and pour the juice into a punch bowl. Stir in the simple syrup.

2. Thinly slice the remaining lemon and place in the bowl. Add 3 cups (720 ml) water and the vodka. Chill for 1 hour.

3. Fill tumbler glasses three-quarters full with ice. Pour in the punch and top with Champagne. Garnish each with a mint sprig down through the glass.

Simple Syrup

MAKES 3 CUPS (720 ML)

---

2 cups (400 g) sugar
2 cups (480 ml) water

In a saucepan, combine the sugar and water. Bring to a boil and simmer for 2 to 3 minutes to dissolve the sugar. Let cool completely, then store in the fridge in an airtight container or a mason jar up to 1 month.

The Sonjarita

The New York ladies are no strangers to tequila. Bethenny even took them to Tequila, Mexico, to see how her margarita empire was made. After an afternoon of tequila-tasting, they weren't feeling any pain poolside as Sonja continued the tasting by downing a pitcher of margaritas and then skinny-dipping with the Skinnygirl herself, Bethenny. The Skinnygirl started it all with her legendary margarita, and we are continuing it with our perfect-for-any-party version. Endearingly called "Sonjarita" by Ramona and Luann, this margarita is in honor of our tequila-loving tipsy girl.

SERVES 8 **PREP TIME:** 10 minutes **TOTAL TIME:** 1 hour 10 minutes (includes 1 hour chilling time)

- 1 (750 ml) bottle good-quality blanco tequila, such as Casamigos
- 2 cups (480 ml) Cointreau
- 1 cup (240 ml) simple syrup (page 207)
- 1 cup (240 ml) fresh lime juice (from 8 to 10 limes; reserve 1 squeezed lime for rubbing the glasses)
- Maldon sea salt
- Lime wheels, for garnish

1. In a large pitcher, combine the tequila, Cointreau, simple syrup, and lime juice. Stir well. Refrigerate for at least 1 hour to chill.

2. Pour some sea salt onto a small plate. Rub the rim of a margarita glass with the reserved lime, and dip the rim of the glass into the salt.

3. Generously fill the glass with ice, top with the chilled margarita mix, and garnish with a lime wheel. If that doesn't float your boat you can always grab the pitcher and drink just like Sonjarita.

Chef Stuart's Tip: Making a pitcher of margaritas is ALWAYS the way to go instead of making individual drinks. This recipe is foolproof. If you want it sweeter, just add more simple syrup.

Amy's Note: Sonja is the straw that stirs the drink, and now she has her *own* drink to stir.

Sweet Tea, Mix It, Jesus

Everybody knows that you're not a true Southern belle if you can't make a perfect sweet tea, and that you're certainly not a good Housewife if you're not "shady." Well, Phaedra has excelled at both, hence the nickname "Shadedra." Phaedra's love for the Lord mixed with a little Southern drama makes for a nice blend, much like our tasty tea. In between being a mother, an attorney, and a funeral director, Phaedra has to take time to have a refreshing sweet tea. After all, she works hard for it! This tea will take you to church. Now cover those knees with a handkerchief and sip away!

SERVES 4 TO 6 **PREP TIME:** 5 minutes **COOK TIME:** 10 minutes **TOTAL TIME:** 1 hour 15 minutes (includes 1 hour chilling time)

---

6 tea bags
½ cup (100 g) sugar
¼ teaspoon baking soda
1 lemon, cut into wedges
Mint sprigs, for garnish

Amy's Note: Perfect for a sip 'n' see or a baptism put on by our favorite party planner, Dwight.

1. In a medium saucepan, bring 2 cups (480 ml) water to a boil. Remove the pan from the heat, add the tea bags, and steep the tea for 10 minutes. Remove the tea bags and add the sugar to the tea, stirring until it has dissolved.

2. Sprinkle the baking soda into a large glass pitcher. Pour the tea into the pitcher, top with 4 cups (960 ml) cold water, and stir.

3. Refrigerate until well chilled, at least 1 hour.

4. Pour the iced tea into tall ice-filled glasses or mason jars, garnish with a lemon wedge and mint sprig, and enjoy.

Chef Stuart's Tip: Fun fact: Adding the baking soda to the pitcher cuts through the bitterness of the tannins in the tea, resulting in a smoother, even more delicious tea.

Green-Eyed Bandits' Booze

You don't want to cross the green-eyed bandits, but you do want to drink like them! Gizelle and Robyn are a loyal duo, and their friendship runs deep. In Potomac, they are a force to be reckoned with and they complement one another—much like the Midori and vodka in this emerald-colored cocktail. This drink is perfect for a mischievous night with your BFF. Enjoy after a pizza delivery prank to your frenemy.

SERVES 1

---

6 mint leaves
½ ounce (15 ml) simple syrup (page 207)
1 ounce (30 ml) Midori liqueur
1 ounce (30 ml) vodka
½ ounce (15 ml) fresh lime juice
Club soda
Mint sprig and lime slice, for garnish

In a cocktail shaker, muddle the mint with the simple syrup. Add the Midori, vodka, lime juice, and ice and shake well. Strain into a tall glass with fresh ice and top with club soda. Garnish with the mint sprig and lime slice.

Amy's Note: Gizelle and Robyn have each other's backs and we've got yours with this radiant and refreshing drink.

Cease and Despritzer

When it comes to legal matters between Housewives, Tamra paved the way. If Tamra didn't walk, Denise Richards wouldn't have run. Tamra was the first to "go there" with a cease and desist letter to Jeana Keough in the Season 6 finale of the OC. Because that's what you do when a cast member talks to the press about your separation, duh. Instead of cooling off with legal papers and a glass of wine to the face, try drinking this refreshing summer spritzer. You won't be "thirsty" for the press anymore!

SERVES 1

---

6 fresh blueberries (frozen work too)
5 ounces (150 ml) red wine (Pinot Noir is best)
2 ounces (60 ml) LaCroix Mixed Berry Sparkling Water
1 mint sprig, for garnish

1. In a large wineglass, lightly crush the blueberries with the back of a wooden spoon.
2. Add ice and the wine, then top with the sparkling water. Garnish with the mint sprig. Enjoy.

Amy's Note: The first wine throw in *Housewives* history will be your go-to summer spritzer.

Lake Bailey 'n' Cream

This smooth after-dinner drink is as sexy and smooth as Cynthia Bailey. A lake house has never looked so good on anyone as it does on our fierce and fabulous Atlanta Housewife, and this drink will make you feel like you're soaking in a bubbly tub at Lake Bailey. When Cynthia bought her lake house we all toasted to her new independence. But it didn't take long for her to meet her soul mate, Mike Hill, while living there. Call it good Irish cream luck! Cynthia has proven that sweetness and success are her superpowers. You are going to feel a sense of romance and delight when this sweet drink hits your lips. You don't have to walk the runway at The Bailey Agency to get to the end of this; just serve face and drink. Sip and #CHill.

SERVES 1

---

1 ounce (30 ml) Baileys Original Irish Cream
1 ounce (30 ml) vanilla vodka, such as Smirnoff
1- to 2-ounce (30 to 60 ml) shot espresso
1 ounce (30 ml) heavy cream
Whipped cream, for garnish
½ shortbread cookie, crumbled, for garnish
1 coffee bean, for garnish

1. Fill a martini glass with ice and water and let sit for 1 minute to chill the glass.

2. Pour out the ice water and pat the glass dry with a paper towel.

3. In a cocktail shaker half-filled with ice, combine the Baileys, vanilla vodka, espresso, and heavy cream and shake for 20 seconds. Strain into the martini glass.

4. Top the drink with whipped cream and sprinkle with the shortbread crumbs and coffee bean.

5. Sit back by the fire and relax—or, if you want to break all the rules, enjoy at your very own "Bailey-Q" or at The Bailey Wine Cellar.

Amy's Note: Enjoy next to a fire while burning your friendship contract.

Go to Sleep Kelly Beantini

You can run in New York City traffic, like Kelly, but you can't hide from Scary Island. Kelly put the Scary in Scary Island, most notably when she was prancing around in her silky purple slip dress eating jelly beans, gummy bears, and lollipops and not making any sense. She yelled at Bethenny because she thought she was going to kill her in her sleep, and Bethenny finally hit her limit and shouted at her to "go to sleep, you're crazy!" Kelly was so taken aback that she was shocked and revolted, and the image of her face lives in our heads rent-free. But we promise you won't make that face when you're drinking this sweet party drink.

---

2 tablespoons purple sanding sugar (available online or in baking stores)
2 ounces (60 ml) citrus vodka
1 ounce (30 ml) Monin lavender syrup
1 ounce (15 ml) fresh lemon juice (reserve the squeezed lemon for rubbing the martini glass)
Jelly beans, 1 lollipop, and gummy bears, for garnish

1. Pour the purple sugar onto a small plate. Rub the rim of a martini glass with the reserved lemon, and dip the rim of the glass into the sugar. In a cocktail shaker half-filled with ice, combine the vodka, lavender syrup, and lemon juice and shake vigorously.

2. Strain into a martini glass. Drop a few jelly beans into the glass if you want and stir with a lollipop. Add gummy bears. AND GO TO SLEEP! GO TO SLEEP!

Amy's Note: Drink before bed to help you sleep or after a photo shoot on the beach. Yohann face!

Lucy Lucy Aperol Spritz Juicy

No one's hands are clean in this and neither will yours be because you have to get a little dirty whether you're making an epic cocktail or an epic reality TV show. The storyline for RHOBH Season 9 was taken over by an unlikely cast member that we never saw . . . a dog named Lucy Lucy Apple Juicy. Yes, it was a pint-size dog that was the cause of the ultimate demise of friendships between LVP and everyone else. We took it hard when LVP didn't show up for the reunion, so we had to drink our sorrows away with this sweet, unsuspecting drink. If you get caught in a lie, just blame it on the spritz.

SERVES 4 TO 6 **PREP TIME:** 10 minutes

¾ cup (180 ml) simple syrup (page 207)
1 (750 ml) bottle sparkling rosé wine
¾ cup (180 ml) Aperol
Juice of 3 lemons
4 cups (960 ml) club soda
1 orange, sliced
Mint sprigs, for garnish

Amy's Note: I did not sell this recipe to *Radar Online* and if you don't believe me, I'm willing to take a lie detector test.

1. Pour the simple syrup into a large pitcher. Add the sparkling wine, Aperol, and lemon juice and stir to combine.
2. Fill large wineglasses three-quarters full with ice. Add the cocktail mix and top with club soda.
3. Garnish each glass with an orange slice and a mint sprig. Enjoy!

Drink Sucked at the Round-Up

Look, we know that when LeeAnne was in her pre-surgery sedated state she was talking all kinds of crazy, but we can't help but wonder whether her foreboding whisper behind that door implicating a certain Dallas house husband of certain sexual shenanigans had the ring of truth to it. . . . In honor of our favorite zonked-out gossipmonger, make this sweet honeysuckle drink whenever you happen to hear a rumor that your honey got suckled at a gay bar! (By the way, Chef Stuart said he got this recipe from a certain someone and I think I know who . . .)

2 ounces (60 ml) honeysuckle vodka
1 ounce (30 ml) whiskey
2 ounces (60 ml) lemonade
Club soda
Orange slice, for garnish

Amy's Note: You don't need knives to make this drink, just hands, and they work quite well.

In a cocktail shaker filled with ice, shake the vodka, whiskey, and lemonade. Strain into a tall glass or mason jar filled with ice, top with club soda, and garnish with an orange slice.

Chef Stuart's Tip: This recipe makes just one cocktail, but you can make a large pitcher to serve a crowd easily. A delicious twist to make it *classy* would be to top this drink with Champagne.

Scepter Peach Nectar Sangria

When the Atlanta peaches hit the couches at the reunions, they never disappoint. But when Miss USA, Kenya, brought props to the reunion to ultimately taunt Porsha, we didn't foresee that an explosive and physical confrontation would ensue—and have to be broken up by Andy Cohen himself! You don't need to brawl over this incredibly delicious drink, though, so put your bullhorn away and use your scepter as a stir stick. Oh, and the Atlanta ladies like it rich, so ditch the sparkling wine and use Champagne, honey; it takes it to another level, like this reunion.

SERVES 4 TO 6 **PREP TIME:** 5 minutes **TOTAL TIME:** 1 hour and 5 minutes (includes 1 hour chilling time)

---

3 cups (710 ml) peach nectar
1 cup (240 ml) peach schnapps
1 (750 ml) bottle Champagne
1 orange, sliced and halved, for garnish
4 strawberries, hulled and sliced, for garnish
Mint sprigs, for garnish

1. In a clear pitcher, combine the peach nectar and schnapps. Refrigerate for 1 hour to chill.

2. Fill large wineglasses with ice. Pour 3 ounces (85 ml) of the nectar/schnapps mixture into each glass and top with Champagne. Garnish with orange slices, strawberry slices, scepter, and mint.

3. Use a megaphone to announce to your party guests that drinks have been served!

Cotton Candy CockTaylor

On a "couples trip" to Vegas, the Beverly Hills gang stayed at Adrienne's hotel, The Palms, where they had an early dinner so that they could make it to the Jay-Z concert in time. They didn't skip dessert and thank the Bravo Gods for that because we got to see Taylor's luscious lips rival the acrobatics of Cirque du Soleil. There was a plethora of sweet treats delivered to their table. Among those were large balls of pink cotton candy that reminded Lisa of her dog, Giggy, so much that she actually cradled the cotton cloud. We're proud to capture Taylor's cotton candy eating technique with this simple party cocktail.

SERVES 1

---

2 ounces (60 ml) vanilla vodka, such as Smirnoff
½ ounce (15 ml) Cointreau
2 ounces (60 ml) unsweetened cranberry juice
½ ounce (15 ml) fresh lemon juice
¾ cup (25 g) cotton candy

Amy's Note: Warning, this drink may be erotic if you consume the cotton candy like Taylor.

1. In a cocktail shaker half-filled with ice, combine the vanilla vodka, Cointreau, cranberry juice, and lemon juice and shake for 20 seconds. Pour into a large chilled martini glass.

2. Float the cotton candy on top and serve while listening to Jay-Z's discography.

Chef Stuart's Tip: Cotton candy can easily be ordered online, and it comes in airtight containers so it can be ordered ahead of time.

Grande Dame Marnier Cosmopolitan

Karen Huger is the self-proclaimed Grande Dame of Potomac, and we celebrate that with a drink that is as high-class and original as she is. Not just a Cosmo, it's made with, of course, Grand Marnier. If you drink enough of these, you may smell notes of her signature perfume, La'Dame Fragrance by Karen Huger. Oh, and because this gorgeous take on a Cosmo is so delicious, we're taking a page from Karen's book and holding a press conference to get the word out.

SERVES 1 **PREP TIME:** 2 minutes **COOK TIME:** 5 minutes **TOTAL TIME:** 17 minutes (includes 10 minutes cooling time)

---

1 ounce (30 ml) rose water simple syrup (recipe follows)
1 ounce (30 ml) fresh lemon juice
1 ounce (30 ml) Grand Marnier
1 ounce (30 ml) unsweetened cranberry juice
2 ounces (60 ml) vodka
Dried edible rose petals, for garnish

In a cocktail shaker filled with ice, combine the simple syrup, lemon juice, Grand Marnier, cranberry juice, and vodka. Shake vigorously and strain into a large martini glass. Garnish with rose petals.

Amy's Note: If you don't enjoy this drink as much as we do, you tacky as hell.

Rose Water Simple Syrup

MAKES 1¼ CUPS (295 ML)

---

1 cup (200 g sugar)
¼ cup (60 ml) Cortas rose water

In a small saucepan, combine the sugar and rose water and cook over medium heat until the sugar has dissolved, about 5 minutes. Let cool completely, then store in the refrigerator in an airtight container or a mason jar up to 1 month.

Chef Stuart's Tip:
You can order both rose water and edible rose petals online. It's worth it!

Dinner Party from Hell PsychicTini

WITH E-CIG

Get your oversize martini glasses and your e-cigs ready because we're off the clock and it's "girls' night." You don't need to "head-tap" us for the recipe, we'll tell you what you need to make your Camille cocktail as amazing and spirited as they looked at her polarizing dinner party from hell. Camille's guest of honor was Alison DuBois, the psychic/medium, who, after some provoking and drinking, was tempted to read Kyle. She didn't hold back, telling Kyle that her husband will never emotionally fulfill her. These PsychicTinis are as close to what we saw in the episode, and just as intoxicating as they appeared. But that's okay, because, as Alison said, "It's a girls' night, so we're not supposed to be good."

SERVES 1

---

1 ounce (30 ml) Monin lavender syrup
4 blueberries, plus more for garnish
1½ ounces (45 ml) vodka
1 ounce (30 ml) St-Germain elderflower liqueur
3 ounces (90 ml) Prosecco

Amy's Note: These drinks are strong and not only will they get you drunk, they will emotionally fulfill you . . . *know that.*

1. In a shaker, muddle the lavender syrup and blueberries together. Add the vodka, elderflower liqueur, and ice. Shake for 20 seconds. Strain into a BIG-ASS martini glass and top with Prosecco.
2. Garnish with 3 blueberries. Sip between drags of your e-cig.

Henny-thing Can Happen

It's no secret that Porsha's drink of choice is Hennessy. She hasn't been shy about drinking it on the show and, fortunately for Porsha, Hennessy is vegan, so she can indulge. When the Atlanta ladies went to Toronto for Carnival, Porsha said she was ready for "Henny-thing to happen." And during the Season 12 virtual reunion, she drank Hennessy the whole time while throwing out some iconic jokes and jabs. Grab a hookah and a Hennessy and jump on a pedal bike with your best friend and pay homage to the Hot Dog Factory.

- 2 ounces (60 ml) Hennessy Cognac
- 2 ounces (60 ml) unsweetened cranberry juice
- ½ ounce (15 ml) fresh lime juice
- 1 lime wheel, for garnish

1. In a cocktail shaker filled with ice, combine the Hennessy, cranberry juice, and lime juice and shake for about 20 seconds.
2. Strain into an ice-filled rocks glass and garnish with the lime wheel.

Long Island OC'd Tea

Our favorite transplant to the OC has brought color and drama, and she has not been shy about sharing her life with us. From a DUI to a divorce to some bad hair choices, Gina has been an outstanding Housewife who has proven that she can turn her life around to make the best out of it. After you make this drink, you can consider yourself "an accomplished woman."

½ ounce (15 ml) gin
½ ounce (15 ml) white rum
½ ounce (15 ml) silver tequila
½ ounce (15 ml) vodka
½ ounce (15 ml) Cointreau
½ ounce (15 ml) simple syrup (page 207)
Orange soda
Orange wedge, for garnish

1. In a cocktail shaker filled with ice, combine the gin, rum, tequila, vodka, Cointreau, and simple syrup and give it a quick shake for about 5 seconds.
2. Pour into a tall glass with the ice.
3. Top with the orange soda and garnish with an orange wedge.

Chef Stuart's Tip: Please use good-quality liquor, such as Hendrick's gin, Bacardi rum, Casamigos tequila, etc., or get ready for the worst hangover ever.

Amy's Note: This drink is not sad or depressing like some say her house is. It's big and tasty!

Make It Nice Spiced Cider

"The Berzerkshires" is a magical place where Dorinda always makes it nice, and our cider recipe conjures the gang's holiday visits to Blue Stone Manor. Dorinda's enthusiastic holiday decorating rivals that of a theme park, featuring life-size mummies, a visit from Santa (herself), and an overabundance of holiday baubles (every kind known to woman). Whether it's yoga, a naked chef, a murder mystery, or "Dor-robics," Dorinda undoubtedly makes a weekend in Great Barrington, well, *great*. In one of her shining moments, she gave a tearful, charged, and exasperated speech on how she bent over backward to make it nice and the women were acting "very poorly," so they should just leave if they couldn't behave themselves. The best thing about this recipe is that it is made in a slow cooker, meaning it will cook all day, giving you plenty of time to decorate and make it nice.

SERVES 6 TO 8 **PREP TIME:** 10 minutes **COOK TIME:** 2 hours 15 minutes
TOTAL TIME: 2 hours 25 minutes

---

1 orange
1 tablespoon whole cloves
2 quarts (1.9 liters) apple cider
¾ cup (75 g) packed light brown sugar
1 teaspoon ground allspice
1 teaspoon ground nutmeg
4 cinnamon sticks, plus more for garnish
1½ cups (360 ml) whiskey

1. Stud the orange all over with the cloves.

2. In a slow cooker, combine the studded orange, cider, brown sugar, allspice, nutmeg, and cinnamon sticks. Cover and set the slow cooker on high for 2 hours.

3. Turn the slow cooker to the warm setting. Stir in the whiskey.

4. Serve in heatproof glasses and enjoy with some extra cinnamon sticks.

Amy's Note: Enjoy with pumpkin pie or birthday cake from Dorinda's mother. Light the candles and put your face in it. If you don't like this cider, you should be ashamed of yourself!

We Got the Yacht Shots

What we wouldn't give to have been a fly on the wall at Lu and Tom's engagement party on the yacht in Palm Beach. Luann welcomed Sonja aboard with open arms and a wink that said, yes, they finally got the yacht back. A giddy Luann looked the other way while Tom's ex-girlfriends, Ramona and Sonja, mingled awkwardly among the eclectic crowd. Fun fact: Tom was also married to Aviva Drescher. So, for those of you keeping score at home, do a shot for every NY Housewife Tom has been with. Make sure you do a toasty toast à la Dorinda. We got the yacht shots! Can you believe it, girls?

4 ounces (120 ml) Bacardi gold rum
1 ounce (30 ml) triple sec
1 ounce (30 ml) fresh lime juice

In a cocktail shaker filled with ice, combine the rum, triple sec, and lime juice and shake well. Strain into shot glasses.

Amy's Note: P.S. The color of these shots is reminiscent of Lu's 8-carat canary-yellow diamond engagement ring. Sorry if it's a little murky.

RECIPE REUNIONS

A Guide to Your Own Housewives Parties

LIKE ANY WORTHWHILE *HOUSEWIVES* REUNION, WE GOT DRESSED TO the nines and took to the couches for a real talk about recipes. We brought our binder of receipts and hashed out which dishes we think are the most dramatic, fun, and polarizing, ensuring that with the right spread, your *Housewives* parties will be truly unforgettable. So have fun and don't be afraid to get theme-y, because we've got you covered, whether you're in the mood to host a premiere party dinner, a beatless brunch, or a Beverly Hills BBQ. Whatever mood you're in, we've got the menu you need to make it a smashing, messy success. This is your moment to host so hold that peach or diamond, or throw a leg! This is your reality.

Stuart and Amy's Watch Party Menus

ORANGE COUNTY

COCKTAIL: 9 Lemons in a Bowl Party Punch **207**

APPETIZER: Tres Amigas 3-Layer Dip **67**

MAINS: Coto de Casserole **109**

Bangin' Meditation Bowl Chicken Paillard **113**

DESSERT: Dubrow-ken Bow Champagne Cupcakes **171**

COCKTAIL: The Singer Stinger Sipper **203**

APPETIZER: Clip Clip Clip Medley of Dips Dips Dips **65**

MAINS: Scary Island Skirt Steak in Jill Zarin-ade **119**

Forgotten Truffle Frois **33**

DESSERT: Life Is a Crème Brûlée **173**

NEW JERSEY

COCKTAIL: A Glug of Ya House Red

MAINS: Prostitution Whore Puttanesca Pasta **149**

Gorga-zola Balls **117**

DESSERT: My Motha's Pizzelle **195**

POTOMAC

Stuart and Amy's *Real Housewives* Party Menus

DINNER PARTY FROM HELL MENU

IS BITCH BETTER? BRUNCH MENU

SLUTTY ISLAND BACHELORETTE MENU

COCKTAILS: Go to Sleep Kelly Beantini **219**

Cotton Candy CockTaylor **227**

APPETIZERS: Hit a Nerve Herb and Tomato Bruschetta **43**

Clip Clip Clip Medley of Dips Dips Dips **65**

Charcuterie Tray "On Display" **68**

I Fly Above, Kandied Wings **45**

DESSERT: Pat the Puss-stacio Cream Pie **175**

SHADY TEA PARTY MENU

COCKTAILS: Sweet Tea, Mix It, Jesus **211**

Lucy Lucy Aperol Spritz Juicy **221**

MAINS: Beatless Brunch Beets and Burrata **97**

Big ChicKim Salad Sandwich **77**

DESSERT: Poop Hat Peach Cobbler **183**

POOL PARTY MENU

COCKTAIL: The Singer Stinger Sipper **203**

APPETIZER: Tres Amigas 3-Layer Dip **67**

MAIN: Sparkle Dogs **55**

DESSERT: Diaper Dump Cake **177**

GAME NIGHT MENU

COCKTAIL: Drink Sucked at the Round-Up **223**

APPETIZERS: Tardy for the Party Mix **47**

Pillow Fight Popcorn Chicken **53**

MAIN: Poker Night Hand-Slapped Pizza **167**

DESSERT: Trash Sprinkle Cookies **185**

BRAVO BRAVO F$*KING DINNER MENU

COCKTAILS: 9 Lemons in a Bowl Party Punch **207**

Grande Dame Marnier Cosmopolitan **229**

APPETIZERS: Housewives Party Platter **70**

Oysters Ramona-feller **131**

MAINS: Who Said That Sesame Salmon **141**

Scary Island Skirt Steak in Jill Zarin-ade **119**

Word on the Street Corn **49**

DESSERT: Ding Dong Dungeon Cake **193**

You Do Not Talk About the Kids Menu

Lest you think Housewives' gatherings are only adult- and alcohol-friendly, we are here to correct you! On the contraire, the Housewives have plenty of love for their kids, whether they're paying attention to them or not. Feel free to spread the joy for the juveniles with these kid-approved creations!

ACKNOWLEDGMENTS

Stuart

I would like to thank my parents and family for their constant support, especially in my moving to the United States, becoming a chef, and following my dreams—and specifically my mom, for getting me in the kitchen when I was a kid, and my dad, who has been such a great cheerleader for my whole journey; and my aunt, for showing me how to be a great baker. My best friend and manager, Jason Pinyan, for always helping me find my way through Hollywood. My friends Chris Garcia, Emily Yeomans, and Craig Gordon. Katherine Latshaw, my fabulous agent at Folio; my editor, Anna Montague, for acquiring the book and for shepherding us through it; Thomas Van Horn, for your constant support over the last two years; Anet Rumberg, for converting my recipes into metric so more people can enjoy this book across the world; my amazing coauthor, Amy Phillips, for making me laugh throughout the writing process and becoming a great friend of mine; and my two Sparkle dogs, Jack and Bo (see page 36), for putting a smile on my face at the end of each day.

Amy

I would like to thank my King, Andy Cohen, for blessing this book with his words and support and for giving us the gift of *The Real Housewives*. Thank you to Bravo TV for your endlessly entertaining programming and to each and every Housewife for the joy and drama that you've given me and especially to those who have embraced the concept that imitation is flattery. Thank you to my darling husband, whose encouragement and humor have always kept me going. To my parents and dear family, whose love and support has made me the wig-wearing, joke-telling author I am today. Huge thanks to Katherine Latshaw and Anna Montague for holding my hand through this process, and while I am used to transforming into a Housewife, they helped transform me into an author. And to Chef Stuart, who invited me to join him on this journey, I will be forever grateful and have some of the greatest memories and recipes from this cookbook. You are without a doubt an incredible chef, Irishman, and friend. To you I say, "chef's kiss."

Production

We would both like to offer our gratitude to the following superstars, who we consider our Dream Team:

Thanks to the incredible focus group who yea'd or nay'd our recipes: Jaime Moyer, Nancy Hayden, Alyssa Heimrich, Jamison Scala, Aliza Rosen, Megan Freeman, and Katie Nahnsen.

Thanks to the miracle-making makeup artist Mayera Abeita, for transforming Amy into each Housewife, flawlessly.

Big thanks to Tammy Wesley at Superstar Hair & Wigs for helping Amy find the perfect wigs.

Special thanks to LaKendra Tookes, for playing the roles of NeNe Leakes and Karen Huger and capturing their characters perfectly and, might we say, stunningly. And for bringing joy and enthusiasm to this process. Find LaKendra at @LaKendraTookes. (See pages 12, 22, and 228.)

Kim Unthank, thank you for giving us the honor of having Roxy the dog play Giggy.

We would also like to thank the following for the amazing job they have collectively done in helping put these beautiful images together:

Angela Boccuzzi Gaines, Food Stylist, Interior
Vanessa Santana, Food Stylist Assistant, Interior
Michael and Aline Hulswit, Food Photography
Breanne Fuller and Lucy Dufala, Food Stylists, Cover Shoot and Food Pages
Riker Brothers, Photography, Cover and Food Pages

INDEX

Note: Page references in *italics* indicate photographs.

C

D

R

S

T

V

W

Y

Z

ABOUT THE AUTHORS

Stuart O'Keeffe is an Irish-born, California-based chef and best-selling author. He appears frequently on TV, starring in Food Network shows such as *Private Chefs of Beverly Hills* and *Let's Eat,* and he has appeared as a judge on *Chopped,* in addition to numerous appearances on *Today* and *Rachael Ray,* where he offers fun, simple recipes to get home cooks into the kitchen. His first cookbook, *The Quick Six Fix,* was released in 2016 by HarperCollins. Stuart received his degree in Culinary Arts from the Dublin Institute of Technology and trained in Bordeaux and the Napa Valley before moving to Los Angeles, where he watches *Housewives* with his two Westies, Jack and Bo. Keep up to date with Stuart at tastybites.net, @Chefstuart on TikTok, @chefstuartokeeffe on Instagram, and Chef Stuart O'Keeffe on Facebook and YouTube.

Amy Phillips is a comedian and radio personality from Grosse Pointe, Michigan, who's currently living her best life in Los Angeles. Amy honed her skills at Wayne State University and at the American Academy of Dramatic Arts in New York City before studying improv at The Second City Detroit and The iO Theater and The Annoyance Theater in Chicago. She combines her love for reality TV and parody with her celebrated *Real Housewives* (and other celeb) imitations, which are a regular feature on Bravo TV's *Watch What Happens Live with Andy Cohen.* Amy currently recaps all things Bravo TV and beyond on her Sirius XM radio show on Radio Andy, *Reality Checked.* Keep up to date with Amy at realamyphillips.com, @meetamyphillips on Instagram, and @AmyPhillips_ on Twitter.